3/92

MINERAL RESOURCES A–Z

Robert L. Bates

✦ *Environment Reference Series* ✦

ENSLOW PUBLISHERS, INC.

Bloy St. & Ramsey Ave.	P.O. Box 38
Box 777	Aldershot
Hillside, N.J. 07205	Hants GU12 6BP
U.S.A.	U.K.

Library of Congress Cataloging-in-Publication Data

Bates, Robert Latimer, 1912-
    Mineral Resources A–Z / Robert L. Bates
    p. cm.—(Environment reference series)
    Includes bibliographical references.
    Summary: A dictionary of terms related to many scientific, technological, and
social problems affecting mineral resources.
    Terms include brines, calcite, flux, groundwater, hardrock mining, mica, and
reclamation.

ISBN 0-89490-244-X

    1. Mines and mineral resources—Dictionaries, Juvenile. [1. Mines and mineral
resources—Dictionaries] I. Title. II. Series.
TN9.B34 1991
553'.03—dc20   90-34301
                                         CIP
                                         AC

Printed in the United States of America

10 9 8 7 6 5 4 3 2 1

ACKNOWLEDGMENT

In preparing the definitions for this book, I have relied heavily on the *Glossary of Geology*, a publication of the American Geological Institute.

CONTENTS

INTRODUCTION 7

TERMS USED IN THE FIELD 11

LAWS AND AGENCIES 23

MINERAL RESOURCE TERMS 27

FOR FURTHER INFORMATION 120

REFERENCES 125

ABOUT THE AUTHOR 128

INTRODUCTION

Mineral resources are substances that we obtain from the earth. They include metals, fuels, construction materials, and industrial minerals. We use enormous amounts of these resources every day in building and highway construction, in running our cars and heating our homes, and in operating our mills and factories.

Big industries have grown up to produce these mineral resources. New oil pools and mineral deposits must be found and developed; the crude oil or the mineral raw material must be refined for use. Care is taken to see that these activities are carried on with minimum damage to the environment. To do all these things successfully is a challenge for industry.

It is helpful to look at the problems connected with mineral resources from a variety of viewpoints. This book demonstrates how science, technology, and society are all involved in mineral-resource issues. This way of looking at the issues will give you a broad base of understanding about our mineral resources and will help you think about the challenge posed by their production, use, and disposal.

Each industry, as you might expect, has its own vocabulary, as do environmentalists. Miners talk about adits and veins; oil people, about wildcats and dry holes; coal producers, about sulfur and Btus. Producers of construction materials refer to overburden or lightweight aggregate. Users of industrial minerals are concerned with anything from abrasives to zircon. The vocabulary of environmental scientists includes radioactive waste, recycling, and pollution.

Mineral Resources A–Z contains definitions of about 250 elements, minerals, rocks, ores, fuels, and related materials. It also includes brief discussions of some of the related problems facing society. A few manufactured products are included, although strictly speaking the mineral industry stops where manufacturing begins. (The mining, milling, and refining of copper is a mineral industry, but making copper wire or tubing is not.)

Subjects defined include the following:

ELEMENTS. For each of about fifty chemical elements: its symbol, a brief description of properties, a statement of uses, and information on the mineral or minerals in which the element is typically found.

MINERALS. Chemical composition in words, and, for many minerals, also in the chemical formula; the properties that make the mineral valuable; its major uses; how and where it is obtained; and any associated health or environmental problems.

ROCKS. Those rocks that are useful because of their physical or chemical properties, where they are found, and how they are extracted and processed.

ORE DEPOSITS AND MINING. Metallic ore, the different types of geological deposits in which it is found, and the methods of mining. Coverage includes crude ore (as mined), the ore mineral (concentrated in a mill), and the metal (refined in a smelter).

MINERAL FUELS. Terms relating to the discovery and production of oil and gas and the various types of deposit; definitions of coal types; and how coal is mined at the surface (strip mining) and underground.

OTHER MATERIALS. Industrial minerals, or nonmetallics; manufactured products; environmental concepts and problems; and related subjects.

REFERENCES. Readers seeking more information will find numbers in parentheses at the end of many of the entries. These are keyed to items in the **References** section.

Also included are sections dealing with:

TERMS USED IN THE FIELD. Definitions of about eighty substances and processes related to the mineral industries that the reader may need to know as background.

LAWS AND AGENCIES. Federal laws and government agencies that deal with the mineral industries, and a note on state regulations.

FOR FURTHER INFORMATION. Addresses of federal and state agencies, public-interest organizations, and trade groups that can furnish more information.

REFERENCES. A list of books and other sources for further reading and used in the preparation of this book.

TERMS USED
IN THE FIELD

ABRASIVES. Granular or powdered substances used in cutting, grinding, and polishing. Natural abrasives include diamond, garnet, sand, and pumice. Examples of manufactured abrasives are carborundum (silicon carbide, SiC), fused alumina (Al_2O_3), and steel shot and grit.

ACID MINE DRAINAGE. Waters flowing from mines and mine wastes where pyrite or other sulfide minerals are exposed to weathering. The sulfides oxidize to produce sulfates and sulfuric acid, which make the water toxic to fish and other stream-dwellers. Acid mine drainage can be decreased or neutralized by treatment with lime.

ALLOY. A mixture of two or more metals. An example is bronze, an alloy of copper and tin. Various ferroalloys are mixtures of iron and another metal, such as chromium or nickel.

ANHYDRITE. A white or light gray sedimentary rock composed of the mineral of the same name, which is calcium sulfate, $CaSO_4$. Anhydrite is the parent material of gypsum and the principal rock in the caprock of salt domes.

11

BASE METAL. Any of the more common and chemically active metallic elements, such as iron, copper, and lead. See also **PRECIOUS METAL.**

BEDROCK. The solid rock that underlies the soil, gravel, or other loose material at the surface.

BRECCIA. A rock made of angular broken rock fragments held together by a mineral cement. Breccias may originate from volcanic explosions, faulting, collapse, or in other ways. Some breccias are the host rock of ore deposits, the ore mineral being present in the cement. Adjective: **BRECCIATED.**

BTU. British thermal unit: the amount of heat required to raise the temperature of one pound of water from 62° F to 63° F (16–17° C). The heating value of coal is given in Btus.

CALCINING. Heating a substance to the temperature at which its constituents separate. For example, calcite ($CaCO_3$) may be calcined to yield CaO (lime) and CO_2 (carbon dioxide).

CARBONATE. A compound consisting of a metal plus CO_3. A series of commercially important carbonate minerals extends from calcium carbonate (calcite, $CaCO_3$) through calcium-magnesium carbonate (dolomite, $CaMg(CO_3)_2$) to magnesium carbonate (magnesite, $MgCO_3$). Limestone and dolomite, rocks composed for the most part of calcite and mineral dolomite respectively, are often referred to as carbonate rocks.

CERAMICS. A general term for objects made chiefly of kaolinitic clay, molded into the desired form and heated or fired in a kiln.

Common ceramics are tile, chinaware, and porcelain. Other raw materials beside clay are feldspar and talc. See also **CERMET.**

CERMET. A tough and heat-resistant mixture of a ceramic and a metal. Cermets are used in such equipment as gas turbines and rocket engines.

CHEMICAL ELEMENT. See **ELEMENT.**

CHERT. A hard and dense sedimentary rock consisting of extremely fine crystals of quartz. Chert tends to break on curved surfaces with sharp edges. It ranges from white and gray to yellow, orange, and brown. See also **FLINT.**

CLEAVAGE. 1. In minerals, the property of breaking along smooth plane surfaces, these being a function of the internal atomic structure of the mineral. 2. In rocks, chiefly slate, the tendency to split into thin sheets in accord with the alignment of platy and flaky minerals.

CORROSION. Chemical wear and tear, such as rusting.

CRYSTAL. A solid body of any element or compound with a regularly repeated internal arrangement of atoms. This arrangement is outwardly expressed by plane faces. Crystals growing into open space may be large and well formed, but commonly, growth is limited by other crystals and the result is a tightly interlocking crystalline body.

DISTILLATION. Heating a substance in order to separate an easily vaporized part from the rest, and then cooling and condensing the vapor to produce a pure or refined product. Oil may be obtained from oil shale by distillation.

DUCTILE. Capable of being stretched, drawn, or hammered without breaking; not brittle. Gold is notably ductile.

ECONOMIC GEOLOGY. The study and analysis of mineral fuels, metallic ore deposits, and nonmetallics; the application of geological knowledge and theory to the search for and the understanding of mineral deposits.

EEZ. See **EXCLUSIVE ECONOMIC ZONE.**

ELEMENT. A substance that cannot be separated into different substances by ordinary chemical means. Elements are the building blocks of minerals. A few elements, for example gold and sulfur, may occur alone in nature, as native elements, but most elements combine with others, as for example silicon and oxygen in the mineral quartz (SiO_2).

EXCLUSIVE ECONOMIC ZONE (EEZ). The waters and the sea bed extending 200 miles off the coasts of the United States and its possessions. This zone was created by presidential proclamation in 1983. All its natural resources are reserved for the United States. Offshore federal lands are administered by the Minerals Management Service of the Department of the Interior, which is responsible for oil and gas leasing as well as exploration for nonfuel minerals.

EXTENDER. Finely ground mineral matter added to paint. Extenders are so-called because their original purpose was to dilute, or extend, expensive pigments. Extenders have now been developed that impart desirable properties to paint, such as increased hiding power, gloss, and brushability. Commonly used extenders include talc, diatomite, and ground calcium carbonate. See also **PIGMENT.**

FAULT. A fracture in rocks along which there has been movement parallel to the fracture surface. Many ore veins are located in fault zones; faults may also serve as traps for oil and gas.

FIBERGLASS. Glass in the form of fine threads, formed by spraying melted glass into cool air. It is used in cloth for draperies, in auto bodies and boat hulls, and in loose fluffy form as heat insulation.

FILLER. Finely ground mineral matter included in such products as paper and plastics. Fillers replace more expensive ingredients and also impart desirable properties to the product. The most commonly used fillers are kaolin, talc, and calcium carbonate.

FLINT. A dark gray or black variety of chert. Nodules of flint have been used in Western Europe as building material and as crushed stone for aggregate.

FLUIDITY. The capacity to flow. Gases and many liquids are highly fluid; viscous liquids are much less so. See also **VISCOSITY.**

FOOL'S GOLD. Pyrite.

FORMATION. In geology, a body of rock, generally layered, that is distinctive and can be recognized over a wide area. For example, a formation called the St. Peter Sandstone yields high-purity sand in Illinois and in Missouri.

GRINDING. The pulverizing of rock material. It may be done to form a desired product, as in grinding marble for filler; or to prepare an ore for processing, as in grinding low-grade copper ore for removal of the metallic mineral. Grinding is commonly done in large rotating steel drums partially filled with steel balls, which break the feed into very fine particles.

HYDROUS. Containing water. Gypsum, $CaSO_4 \cdot 2H_2O$, is a hydrous mineral.

HYDROXYL. A radical, OH, present in all hydroxides.

IGNEOUS ROCKS. Rocks formed by the cooling and solidification of magma. Igneous rocks are made of silicate minerals. An example is lava. See also **METAMORPHIC ROCKS** and **SEDIMENTARY ROCKS.**

IMPERMEABILITY. The condition of a rock, sediment, or soil that makes it incapable of transmitting a fluid.

IMPERMEABLE. Not capable of allowing passage of a fluid.

INERT. Not active; not combining chemically with other substances, or without power to resist an opposing physical force.

INORGANIC. Not made of material with an animal or vegetable origin; derived from mineral sources. See also **ORGANIC.**

KILN. An oven in which freshly formed bricks, pottery, or other ceramic materials are heated in order to change their internal structure by partial melting.

LAVA. An informal term that applies both to molten rock material that flows out onto the earth's surface and to the solid rocks formed from it.

MAGMA. Molten silicate fluid within the earth's crust, before loss of gases or other constituents. Magma is the parent material of igneous rocks. Adjective: **MAGMATIC**.

METALLURGY. The techniques of separating metals and metallic minerals from their ores by mechanical and chemical processes.

METAMORPHIC ROCKS. Rocks that have been formed from preexisting rocks by heat, pressure, and the action of hot vapors or solutions in the earth's crust. Examples are slate (from shale), marble (from limestone), and quartzite (from sandstone). See also **IGNEOUS ROCKS** and **SEDIMENTARY ROCKS**.

MIGRATION. The movement of water, ore-forming fluids, oil, or gas through the rocks of the earth's crust.

MINERAL. A naturally occurring solid inorganic substance that has an orderly internal structure and characteristic chemical composition, crystal form, and physical properties. Minerals are the constituents of rocks and of ore deposits. Used as an adjective, as in mineral resources, the term refers to all earth-derived materials of value—metals, non-metals, and fuels.

NATIVE ELEMENT. A chemical element that is found as a mineral in nature, uncombined with other elements. Examples are sulfur and gold.

ORGANIC. A term referring to compounds that contain carbon. In a general sense, organic materials are of animal or vegetable origin. Coal and petroleum are examples. See also **INORGANIC**.

OXIDATION. The union of a substance with oxygen.

PELLETIZING. Combining powdery iron ore with bentonite to form small rounded masses, or pellets, for ease in handling and shipping.

PERMEABILITY. The capacity of a porous rock to allow a fluid to move through it. Permeability depends on the size of the pore spaces and the extent to which they are connected. A rock may be very porous but have little or no permeability (for example, pumice); the reverse is not possible. See also **POROSITY.**

PERMEABLE. Allowing the movement or migration of fluids.

PETROCHEMICALS. A general term for hundreds of chemical compounds that are made from petroleum. A common example is paraffin. Industrial plants that make petrochemicals are potential sources of air and water pollution.

PIG IRON. Iron in molten form as it comes from the blast furnace. It is cast into forms called pigs.

PIGMENT. Fine powder, either a mineral or a mineral-derived product, that gives paint its color and its ability to hide previous coats. Pigments make up about 18 percent of the raw materials used in paint manufacture. See also **EXTENDER.**

POROSITY. The percentage of the bulk volume of a rock that is occupied by voids, of whatever size, whether isolated or connected. Examples are pumice and loosely cemented sandstone. See also **PERMEABILITY.**

POROUS. Containing voids or open spaces.

PRECIOUS METAL. A general term for gold, silver, and metals of the platinum group. See also **BASE METAL.**

PUBLIC DOMAIN. Lands that have always been under federal ownership, plus lands obtained by the government through purchase or exchange.

RADICAL. In chemistry, a group of two or more atoms that acts as a single atom and goes through a reaction unchanged. An example is hydroxyl, OH.

RADIOACTIVITY. The emission of radiant energy in the form of particles or rays when unstable atomic nuclei change to a more stable form. Radioactivity is a property of uranium, thorium, and a few other elements. It is utilized in the form of atomic energy. Particles emitted in radioactivity damage cells in the human body and can cause cancer and genetic defects.

REFRACTORIES. Substances that are resistant to high temperatures. Some refractories are minerals, for example chromite and graphite; others are rocks, such as quartzite; and some are manufactured products, as refractory bricks and magnesia. Refractories are required in the production of metals, glass, ceramics, cement, and any other material whose processing calls for great heat.

REPLACEMENT. In nature, the removal of mineral matter in solution and the simultaneous deposition of another mineral in its place. Replacement is an important ore-forming process, as for example in the formation of fluorspar deposits by replacement of limestone.

ROCK. An aggregate of minerals. Granite, sandstone, and marble are examples. Exceptions to the definition include volcanic glasses, such as pumice and perlite, which are not differentiated into minerals; and coal, which consists of organic material.

SEDIMENTARY ROCKS. Rocks formed by consolidation of clay, sand, shell fragments, or other sediments; by precipitation of dissolved salts from a water body that dries up; or by the accumulation of plant matter. Sedimentary rocks—limestone, sandstone, salt, gypsum, coal—are extremely important in industry. See also **IGNEOUS ROCKS** and **METAMORPHIC ROCKS**.

SEMICONDUCTOR. A substance whose conductivity is poor at low temperatures but is improved by slight additions of other substances or by heat, light, or voltage. A mercury-cadmium-tellurium semiconductor is the principal photoconductive material used in making infrared images of the land surface from space.

SILICATE. A mineral containing SiO_4 in its crystal structure, combined with one or more metallic elements. An example is olivine, $(Mg,Fe)_2SiO_4$. The minerals of igneous rocks and of most metamorphic rocks are silicates.

SILICEOUS. Containing abundant silica, in free form rather than as silicates. Chert and quartzite are examples of highly siliceous rocks.

SPECIFIC GRAVITY. The ratio of the weight of a given volume of a substance to the weight of an equal volume of water. For example, quartz, with a specific gravity of 2.65, is 2.65 times as heavy as water. Abbreviation: **sp. gr.**

STEEL. A hard, tough metallic material made of iron with a small percentage of carbon, often alloyed with nickel, chromium, or other metals to impart special properties.

SULFATE. A compound consisting of a metal plus SO_4. An example is calcium sulfate, $CaSO_4$, the mineral anhydrite.

SULFIDE. A compound consisting of a metal plus sulfur. An example is iron disulfide, FeS_2, the mineral pyrite.

SUPERCONDUCTOR. A metal or alloy that will conduct electric current without resistance when cooled to temperatures near absolute zero (-273.15° C or -459.67° F). Scientists are trying to develop materials that will act as superconductors at much higher temperatures.

SYNTHETIC. In the mineral industry, a term meaning artificial or manufactured; not natural.

VISCOSITY. In a fluid, the quality of being thick, syrupy, and slow-flowing. Viscosity is a result of internal fluid resistance caused by molecular attraction. Adjective: **VISCOUS.** See also **FLUIDITY.**

WEATHERING. The mechanical and chemical changes that rocks undergo on long exposure to air, water, and organic matter.

LAWS AND AGENCIES

GENERAL MINING LAW OF 1872. This declares minerals on lands owned by the government to be free and open to exploration and purchase. It authorizes mining claims to be located by a procedure that is largely unchanged to this day. Should a discovery be made, the site must be physically marked, or located, to indicate boundaries, and a notice must be posted. A claim can then be filed at the nearest courthouse or Bureau of Land Management office. Since 1976, all claims under the 1872 Mining Law must be recorded annually with the Bureau of Land Management.

MINERAL LEASING ACT OF 1920. Under this act certain materials were withdrawn from disposal under the Mining Law and were made available through a leasing system. These materials include coal, oil and gas, oil shale, and phosphates, among others.

MATERIALS ACT OF 1947. This authorized the sale of sand, stone, gravel, and common clay on public lands.

The Mining Law of 1872 and the acts of 1920 and 1947 form the legal framework for mining in the United States. How much these laws have had to be revised, amended, and interpreted may be judged from the fact that the *Handbook of Mineral Law* is 700 pages in length.

WILDERNESS ACT OF 1964. This created a national system of wilderness on federally owned land. These lands were open to development for twenty years, but since 1983 they have been off limits to mining.

NATIONAL ENVIRONMENTAL AND POLICY ACT OF 1970. This act established the Environmental Protection Agency (EPA). It requires that any proposal for an activity that may affect the environment must include a detailed statement of the impact to be expected. Such an Environmental Impact Statement has become a significant part of any proposal to open a new mine or extend an old one. See also **ENVIRONMENTAL IMPACT STATEMENT.**

SURFACE MINING CONTROL AND RECLAMATION ACT OF 1977. This act requires reclamation of all surface mines for coal. The land must be restored to a useful form and as nearly as feasible to its original contours.

FEDERAL MINE SAFETY AND HEALTH AMENDMENTS ACT OF 1977. This act placed the responsibility for enforcing mine health and safety laws on the Mine Safety and Health Administration (MSHA) of the Department of Labor.

OTHER LAWS. Several Acts of Congress, not directed specifically at the mineral industries, may affect mining operations. Among these are the Clean Air Act of 1990, the Clean Water Act of 1972, and the Endangered Species Act of 1973.

U.S. BUREAU OF MINES. This agency of the Department of the Interior is concerned with the extraction, properties, and uses of mineral resources. One of its publications, the *Minerals Yearbook,* is the primary source of statistical information on the mineral industries.

U.S. GEOLOGICAL SURVEY. This agency of the Interior Department is a science and research organization, involved mainly in geological studies, exploration, mapping, and conservation. Its publications and maps are basic sources of information on mineral resources.

STATE LAWS AND REGULATIONS. Mining on privately owned or state-owned land may take place by agreement between the landowner and the mining company. Such mining is subject not only to federal laws on clean water, clean air, and the like, but also to state, country, and municipal regulations on such matters as land use, noise, and truck traffic. Mining today is a closely regulated industry.

MINERAL
RESOURCE TERMS

A

ADIT. A horizontal passage from the ground surface into a mine. It is sometimes called an entry or a tunnel.

AGGREGATE. Sand, gravel, crushed stone, or other hard granular material used in construction and highway building. Most aggregate is mixed with cement to form concrete, or with asphalt for blacktop paving material. The total tonnage of aggregate produced per year is far greater than that of any other mineral resource. See also **LIGHTWEIGHT AGGREGATE.** (3, 5)

ALUMINA. Another name for aluminum oxide (Al_2O_3), the compound from which aluminum is made. It is the intermediate stage in the refining of aluminum from bauxite. Alumina is useful as a refractory and an abrasive.

ALUMINUM (Al). A lightweight metallic element that is easily worked and resists corrosion. Aluminum is used in a wide range of products, from beer cans and kitchen utensils to electrical wiring and jet aircraft. Over 5 million tons is consumed in the United States each year. The chief ore of aluminum is bauxite. To obtain one pound of aluminum from bauxite requires six kilowatt-hours of electricity—enough to power a 1000-watt bulb for six hours. In 1987 the industry obtained nearly 16 percent of its raw-material needs from recycled aluminum cans at a great saving of electrical energy. See also **BAUXITE.** (8)

ANTHRACITE COAL. Hard black coal whose carbon content exceeds 90 percent. It has a high heating value and burns with a short blue flame and no smoke. See also **COAL.**

ANTIMONY. (Sb, from the Latin *stibium*). A silvery white metallic element. The use of antimony oxide as a flame retardant is the dominant market. Antimony is obtained either as a byproduct in the smelting of lead ore or from the sulfide mineral stibnite, Sb_2S_3. Metallic antimony is inert, but some of its gaseous compounds are injurious to skin, eyes, and lungs. Conditions in smelting and processing plants are closely monitored.

APATITE. A group of minerals consisting of calcium phosphate, $Ca_5(PO_4)_3$, with varying amount of fluorine, chlorine, carbonate, or hydroxyl. Apatite is the valuable part of phosphate rock. It is also present in bones and teeth. See also **PHOSPHATE ROCK.**

ARSENIC (As). A silvery white metallic element that is highly toxic. About 75 percent is used in copper arsenate, a wood preservative, and about 20 percent in weedkillers and other agricultural chemicals. Gallium arsenide is a good semiconductor. Arsenic is a byproduct of lead refining. All arsenic used in the United States is imported. Several compounds of arsenic are extremely toxic. Exposure in the workplace may lead to cancer of the skin, the lungs, and the liver. See also **GALLIUM.**

ARTIFICIAL BRINE. Salt-laden water produced in solution mining. See also **SOLUTION MINING.**

ASBESTOS. A general name for several silicate minerals that readily separate into strong, flexible fibers. Combined with cotton or rayon, fibers one-half inch long or more can be spun into yarn and woven into cloth. Heat-resistant and noninflammable, this cloth is used in such products as brake linings, fireproof theater curtains and scenery, and safety clothing. Short asbestos fibers are used in compressed or molded products in which the fibers are held firmly in resin or other material acting as a binder. Products include ceiling tile, floor tile, asbestos-cement pipe, and paper. About 95 percent of commercial asbestos is the mineral chrysotile, a silicate of magnesium. Chrysotile is the only asbestos mineral mined in North America. The leading source is the Thetford district, south of Quebec City in Canada. Here the mineral occurs in thin veinlets in a dark green metamorphic rock. The rock is crushed, freeing the fibers, which are then whisked off by means of air suction.

In the past, workers in factories, shipyards, and other industrial sites spent their days in a haze of dust, some of which was asbestos. Many contracted lung disease, which unfortunately did not show up until late in their lives. Dangerous conditions in most workplaces have now been corrected, but people have tended to conclude that asbestos products are hazardous to the health of the general public. This conclusion is clear in rulings of the Environmental Protection Agency (EPA). In 1989 the EPA announced that nearly all asbestos products in this country were to be banned by 1997. Such a ban naturally means that substitutes must be found for asbestos in its many applications. Much research has gone into this problem. The substitutes so far proposed, such as fiberglass, cellulose, and steel fibers, are less efficient than asbestos, and they cost more. Furthermore, some of them may themselves be hazardous.

The fact remains that exposure to chrysotile asbestos does not create health risks unless the mineral is breathed as dust for long periods of time. The asbestos fibers in construction materials in schools and other public buildings are held in cement, synthetic resin, or other binder. If they are not free to float in the air they pose no health hazard. (2, 5)

ASH. In coal, the inorganic material that does not burn and is thus left after combustion.

ASPHALT. Brown to black organic matter, solid or stiffly liquid, that is formed in oil-bearing rocks at or near the surface when the gas and light-oil fractions evaporate. It is used mainly in road paving. Asphalt is mined in Trinidad; it is also manufactured from coal or petroleum.

B

BARITE. A white or gray mineral, chemical name barium sulfate ($BaSO_4$). It is exceptionally heavy for a nonmetallic mineral, having a specific gravity of 4.5. Finely ground, barite is used as a weighting agent in oil-well drilling fluid to guard against dangerously high gas pressures. Barite also serves as a filler in paper, paint, and textiles. The major U.S. source is the Battle Mountain area of Nevada, where beds of barite occur with layers of chert and siliceous shale. It is possible that these beds were formed when hydrothermal solutions poured out onto the floor of a sea in the Devonian age, some 360 million years ago. See also **WHITE SMOKER.** (2)

BASALT. A dark, heavy igneous rock that occurs as consolidated lava flows, or in sheetlike bodies that cooled and hardened near the surface and are now exposed by erosion. Dense and fine-grained, basalt is crushed for use as aggregate in concrete. It is known in commerce as traprock. Deposits near urban markets are important in the New Jersey/New York/Connecticut region. Extensive basalt deposits are also found in Oregon and Washington State.

BAUXITE. A white, buff, or yellowish earthy rock composed of aluminum oxides and hydroxides mixed with sand, clay, and iron oxides. About 95 percent is used as an ore of aluminum. The remainder is calcined or fused in the manufacture of refractories, abrasives, and aluminum chemicals. Bauxite deposits are formed by the prolonged weathering of aluminum-rich rocks, such as granite, in a hot, humid climate. There are important deposits in Guyana and Surinam, South America; Guinea, West Africa; Queensland, Australia; and mainland China. There is modest production of bauxite in central Arkansas.

BENTONITE. A group of light-colored clays with various special properties. When one type of bentonite is finely ground and added to water, the clay particles separate, producing a gel or suspension that will not settle out. This property accounts for bentonite's largest use, in oil-well drilling fluids. Bentonite is also used as a binder in molding sands that receive molten metal, and in forming powdered iron ore into pellets for ease in handling. Absorbent bentonite is used in pet litter, as an anti-caking agent, and as a carrier in managing hazardous chemicals. Bentonite is a product of the weathering and alteration of volcanic ash. It is mined from flat-lying near-surface beds in Wyoming and Montana, in a district on the Florida-Georgia line, and in several foreign countries. (5)

BERYLLIUM (Be). A metallic element found in combination with other elements. Most of the metal produced goes into beryllium-copper alloys, for use in computer parts, electrical relays, aircraft bearings, and other specialized products. The major ore mineral of beryllium is bertrandite. This mineral, a beryllium silicate, occurs as tiny crystals throughout certain beds of volcanic ash in western Utah. A minor source of the metal is beryl, a coarsely crystalline silicate mineral that occurs in some pegmatites. Emerald and aquamarine are gem varieties of beryl.

Mists, dusts, and fumes of beryllium are harmful to the skin and lungs, and all persons handling the metal must adopt safety equipment and procedures. The industry has imposed rigid control methods.

BISMUTH (Bi). A grayish white metallic element. Though produced in small quantities, it has a variety of uses in the pharmaceutical and chemical industries. An alloy containing bismuth melts at a low temperature and is used in automatic fire-alarm and sprinkler systems. Bismuth is a byproduct of the refining of lead ores.

BIT. The tool that cuts the hole in rock being drilled. Bits are of varying sizes and designs, as for taking cores or for drilling rocks of differing hardnesses.

BITUMINOUS COAL. Black, banded coal that has a high heating value and burns with a smoky flame. Also known as soft coal, it is the most abundant and commercially valuable coal type. See also **COAL** and **HIGH-SULFUR COAL.**

BLACK GRANITE. A commercial term for any dark igneous rock that will take a polish. The Vietnam Memorial in Washington, D.C., is made of black granite from India.

BLACK SMOKER. A vent in the sea floor, from which a jet of hot dark water gushes into the ocean. The water, black with sulfide minerals, has a temperature of at least 350° C (662° F) and flows out at a rate of 3 to 16 feet (1 to 5 meters) per second. The mineral matter comes to rest nearby and forms a layer of sulfide-rich sediment. Some ore deposits may have originated from black smokers in ancient seas. See also **WHITE SMOKER.**

BLIND DEPOSIT. A mineral deposit that is not exposed at the earth's surface. Oil and gas pools are blind deposits, but the term generally refers to bodies of metallic ore. For example, a gold deposit some two thousand feet (610 meters) below the snowy wastes of the Yukon Territory in Canada is being mined. Blind deposits are found by geological and geophysical surveys, followed by exploratory drilling.

BONANZA. A miner's term for a rich body of ore or a rich part of a deposit. The word is Spanish and means prosperity or success.

BORATES. A group of white translucent minerals occurring in crystalline masses. Borax, the most important, is a sodium borate with ten molecules of water: $Na_2B_4O_7 \cdot 10H_2O$. The world's largest borax deposit is found at shallow depth in the bed of a dried-up lake in the Mojave Desert of California. Another borate mineral, colemanite, is a calcium borate: $Ca_6B_6O_{11} \cdot 5H_2O$. It has long been imported from Turkey, but in 1987 a company was developing a technology for the solution mining of colemanite in California. Borates are used in glassmaking, especially in heat-resistant glass like Pyrex, and in soaps, detergents, and chemicals such as boric acid. (2)

BRINES. A general term for waters with abnormally large amounts of dissolved mineral matter. Natural brines include seawater, which can be evaporated to yield salt; waters recovered by deep wells, which may yield bromine and iodine; and waters saturating the rocks below the surface of dried-up desert lakes, which produce compounds of potassium, sodium, lithium, and other soluble elements. See also **SOLUTION MINING.**

BROMINE (Br). An element that is a liquid at room temperature, but readily changes to a red vapor that is extremely irritating to the eyes, nose, and throat. Its odor is well described by its name, which comes from the Greek *bromos,* meaning stench. Bromine is used in ethylene dibromide for gasoline, and in pesticides, dyes, and other chemicals. Most bromine comes from deep-well brines in Arkansas and Michigan.

BROWN COAL. Lignite.

C

CADMIUM (Cd). A bluish-white, soft metallic element used in metal plating, batteries, pigments, and low-melting alloys. In the late 1980s cadmium was being applied in developing superconductors. It is produced commercially as a byproduct in the smelting of zinc concentrates. Cadmium is toxic when inhaled or ingested.

CALCITE. A common white to gray mineral, chemical name calcium carbonate ($CaCO_3$). Calcite is the chief mineral of limestone, marble, and chalk; a common cementing agent in sandstone; and a gangue mineral in ore deposits. See also **GANGUE.**

CAPROCK. An irregular layer of rock, mostly anhydrite, at the top of a salt dome; it lies between the salt below and the sediments above. Some caprocks include layers of broken, cavernous limestone containing native sulfur. Other caprocks contain oil and gas. See also **SALT DOME.** (5)

CASING. Steel pipes placed in an oil or gas well to support the walls of the hole, prevent loose rock from caving in, and shut off unwanted water.

CEMENT. 1. A gray powder which, when mixed with water, makes a plastic mass that will set to rocklike hardness. Together with aggregate, it makes concrete. The cement industry is very large. In 1987, a total of forty-five companies operated plants in forty-one states to produce over 74 million tons of cement. This output was valued at $4.5 billion. In addition, the United States imported some 18 million tons of cement (up from 4 million tons in 1983). Foreign companies, especially in Western Europe, owned 54 percent of United States production capacity, an increase from 22 percent in 1983.

About 80 percent of the raw material of cement is limestone, the remainder being shale. These materials are crushed, carefully blended, and ground to a powder. This is then fed into the upper end of a slightly inclined rotary kiln, which is a steel tube lined with refractory bricks. Some of these kilns are as much as 25 feet (7.6 meters) in diameter and 500 feet (152 meters) long; they are the largest single units of moving machinery in industry. The charge moves gradually down the kiln under gravity, toward the lower end, where an intense heat is produced by combustion of oil, gas, or powdered coal. Tongues of flame may reach 30 to 40 feet (9 to 12 meters) into the kiln. In the heat blast, at a maximum temperature of about 1500° C (2730° F), the kiln charge is partially melted, and it emerges as a glassy clinker composed of silicates and aluminates. After cooling, the clinker is mixed with 2 to 4 percent of gypsum, to regulate setting time, and is ground extremely fine. The resulting powder is cement.

Research is being done on improving the durability and strength of cement, by adding such things as compounds to reduce porosity, and steel needles to help bind the mass more firmly. 2. In geology, any naturally occurring mineral matter that binds grains together to form sedimentary rock. (3, 5)

CESIUM (Cs). A silver-white metallic element that is extremely reactive in air, water, and other mixtures. A small amount, all of which is derived from an imported ore mineral, is used in research and development, and in photoelectric and other products. The high reactivity and high cost of cesium limit its applications. The properties of cesium and its compounds are identical to those of rubidium. See also **RUBIDIUM.**

CHALK. 1. A soft white earthy limestone, consisting of minute shells made by microscopic floating organisms. Chalk is typically more than 90 percent calcite; in some beds, potato-size nodules of flint are common. Chalk is the rock of the famous White Cliffs of Dover. Ground very fine, chalk is used as a filler. 2. Ordinary blackboard chalk. This is a manufactured product containing gypsum.

CHEMICAL RAW MATERIALS. An inclusive term for minerals and rocks used in the chemical industry. The big four are salt, lime, sulfur, and coal (or petroleum). Many other earth materials are used in small amounts.

CHROMIUM (Cr). A grayish white hard metallic element that has a high resistance to corrosion. More than half the output goes into stainless steel. Chromium chemicals are used in leather tanning and in the pigment chrome yellow, $PbCrO_4$. The only significant source of chromium is the mineral chromite, $(Fe,Mg)(Cr,Al)_2O_4$, which is itself used in refractories. Most of the world's chromite comes from South Africa and the U.S.S.R., so that assuring supplies for the United States is a politically sensitive matter. Certain chromium compounds are poisonous, destroying red corpuscles in the blood and injuring the digestive tract.

CHRYSOTILE. See ASBESTOS.

CLAY. A naturally occurring earthy substance that has extremely fine (submicroscopic) particle size, an essential composition of the clay minerals, and commonly some plasticity when moist. Clays contain impurities such as quartz grains, iron oxide, and organic matter. See also **BENTONITE, CLAY MINERALS,** and **KAOLIN.** (3, 5)

CLAY MINERALS. A complex group of extremely fine-grained minerals. They are essentially hydrous silicates of aluminum; in some varieties magnesium and iron are present. Magnified many hundred times, clay particles are seen to have a platy or flaky character, much like that of the micas (to which they are related). Clay minerals are formed chiefly by long-continued weathering of primary silicate minerals, especially feldspar. The most abundant clay minerals are kaolinite (in kaolin), smectite (in bentonite), and illite (in common clay and shale).

COAL. A dark brown to black combustible sedimentary rock, made chiefly of carbonized plant remains. Most of the plants that formed coal grew in swamps. Dead branches, leaves, and other plant parts fell into acidic stagnant water, which kept them from complete decay. Coal formation starts with a bed of water-saturated peat, which is eventually buried by younger sediments. Deeper burial expels the water, and starts to drive off the oxygen, hydrogen, and other volatile matter from the vegetation. Lignite, also called brown coal, is produced as the first step, or rank, above peat in the coal series. Disregarding ash (unburnable minerals) and moisture, lignite has a volatile-matter content of about 48 percent, the remainder being fixed carbon. The next rank is bituminous or soft coal. This rank covers a broad part of the series and is by far the most valuable and widely used rank of coal. A typical bituminous coal contains about 27 percent volatile matter. In anthracite, or hard coal, the volatile matter is down to about six percent. In graphite, the logical final rank in the series, volatile matter is zero and fixed carbon is 100 percent. This material won't burn and is no longer coal.

Coal of any rank contains mineral matter, or ash. In a four-part analysis (moisture, ash, volatile matter, fixed carbon), the ash content of commercial coal is 2 to 12 percent. Coal's heating value is expressed in British thermal units (Btu) per pound. Lignite has a heating value of about 7,000 Btu; a typical bituminous coal nearly twice as much, 13,530 Btu; and anthracite, 13,130 Btu. Besides being a source of heat, coal is a chemical raw material of great value.

The rank of a coal reflects its geologic history. Beds of low-rank lignite have been undisturbed by earth forces since deposition, and are at or near the surface. Bituminous coals are older and have been deeply buried and compacted by the weight of overlying sediments. Anthracite coal has been produced by folding and squeezing of the sedimentary rocks in mountain-building. Rocks containing graphite have been so tightly sheared and recrystallized that they are no longer sedimentary but metamorphic rocks.

Coal is mined both at the surface and underground. The dust produced in underground coal mining, if breathed by miners over a long period of time, may cause the disease called black lung. This leads to chest pains and extreme shortness of breath. Black lung has long been regarded as a job hazard for coal miners in Kentucky, West Virginia, and other Appalachian coal-producing states. See also **COAL TAR, COKE, HIGH-SULFUR COAL, LONGWALL MINING,** and **STRIP MINING.** (11)

COAL TAR. A thick black viscous liquid obtained from the destructive distillation of bituminous coal to make coke. It is the parent material of many products, including dyes, medicines, explosives, moth balls, and wood preservatives.

COBALT (Co). A hard gray metallic element. A major use is in superalloys for aircraft engines. A radioactive variety, Co-60, is used in the treatment of cancer. Cobalt is a byproduct of copper and nickel mining. The United States imports cobalt from Zaire and Zambia in Africa and from Canada.

COKE. The gray porous residue left after bituminous coal is heated in the absence of air to 900°–1200° C (1650°–2200° F), so as to drive off the volatile matter. Coke has a high carbon content and burns with intense heat and little smoke. Coke is used chiefly in steelmaking. The volatile matter is recovered in the form of coal tar.

COLUMBIUM. An old name for **NIOBIUM.**

CONCENTRATES. In ore processing, the ore mineral after separation from the gangue. Concentrates are conveyed to the smelter. The mine produces ore; the mill produces concentrates; and the smelter produces the metal.

CONCRETE. A mixture of cement with sand, gravel, crushed stone, or other aggregate. It is essential in practically all building and highway construction. (3)

CONTINENTAL SHELF. That part of the continent extending from the shoreline seaward to a depth of about 650 feet (200 meters). Its surface slopes seaward very gently, at a rate of about ten feet per mile. Some areas of the continental shelf, as along the Gulf Coast of the United States, are the sites of offshore drilling for oil and gas. Two areas, offshore from Boston and New York, are known to contain large minable deposits of sand and gravel at shallow depths; they may be mined in the future. Government regulations for marine mining, including environmental safeguards, were being developed in 1989, and dredging could start within five years. Local disturbances of marine life will be inevitable, but pollution should be minor. See also **EXCLUSIVE ECONOMIC ZONE** and **OFFSHORE DEPOSIT.**

COPPER. (Cu, from the Latin *cuprum*). A reddish brown metallic element. It can be hammered or pressed into various shapes and is an excellent conductor of heat and electricity. The major uses are in wire and electrical equipment, pipes and tubes, and roofing. Alloyed with zinc, copper forms brass. The American five-cent piece is only about 25 percent nickel, the remainder being copper.

Copper is the only metal that is found in native form in large masses such as branching aggregates, sheets, or plates filling narrow cracks in the host rock. Although it was once an important ore, native copper no longer interests mining companies. Some of the world's largest copper deposits are low-grade porphyry deposits, which contain no more than one or two percent copper. Immense open-pit mines have been developed in deposits of this type in Arizona, Utah, and New Mexico, as well as in Chile. The chief ore mineral, disseminated in fine grains, is chalcopyrite, $CuFeS_2$. Other important sulfide minerals are chalcocite, Cu_2S, and bornite, Cu_5FeS_4. The porphyry containing these minerals is mined in bulk, crushed, and put through grinding mills. The ore minerals are then concentrated by flotation or other means. In mining districts where copper sulfide minerals occur in vein systems, the upper, near-surface parts of the veins may contain a different set of minerals, the result of long-continued weathering. These include an oxide, cuprite, Cu_2O, and two brightly colored carbonate minerals, azurite, $Cu_3(CO_3)_2(OH)_2$, and malachite, $Cu_2CO_3(OH)_2$. Azurite is deep blue and is not only an ore mineral but also a semiprecious stone. Malachite is bright green, often banded in different shades, and is used to make ornamental objects. See also **PORPHYRY DEPOSITS.** (8)

CORING. A method of drilling, using a pipelike bit that cuts a ring-shaped hole. A cylindrical core of rock rises within the bit as drilling proceeds. Cores tell the geologist what rocks are below ground and whether valuable ore minerals are present. Coring is a routine practice in mining operations. It is also used in the early exploration stages for oil and gas.

CRUDE OIL. Liquid petroleum as it comes from the well. In the industry it is sometimes referred to simply as crude. See also **ENVIRONMENTAL IMPACT.**

CRUSHED STONE. Rock crushed and screened into size grades, mostly for use as aggregate in concrete. Crushed stone also forms the bottom layer, or base course, of highways. Limestone and dolomite are the most widely used; other rocks in common use are basalt (traprock) and granite. The type used depends largely on local availability. (3)

D

DEPLETION. The gradual using up or exhaustion of a mineral deposit. Every ton of ore or barrel of oil produced not only provides income for the operator but also decreases his capital by depleting the deposit. New deposits must be found to replace depleted ones. See also **DEPLETION ALLOWANCE.**

DEPLETION ALLOWANCE. A portion of a mineral producer's income deducted before his taxes are calculated, to protect the business against exhaustion of capital. For example, the depletion allowance for domestically produced iron ore is 12 percent, that for oil and gas is 15 percent. See also **DEPLETION.**

DEPOSIT. See **ORE DEPOSIT.**

DESULFURIZATION. The removal of sulfur from smokestack gases at plants generating electric power. There are several methods. In the fluidized-bed method, controlled burning of coal takes place in a bed of granular dolomite or limestone; this alkaline material absorbs sulfur oxides, preventing their release to the stack. In the scrubbing method, the stack gases are passed through a mist containing pulverized lime or limestone that traps the sulfur gas. The sulfurous material resulting from these processes may be discarded as waste or treated for the production of sulfur or sulfuric acid.

DEVELOPMENT. The preparation of a newly discovered mineral deposit for commercial production, as by building an access road, sinking a shaft, and preparing a mill site.

DIAMOND. A mineral, one of two naturally occurring forms of the element carbon (symbol: C), the other being graphite. Diamond is valued as a gemstone because of its clarity and brilliance. In industry, its value lies in its hardness. Diamond is the hardest natural substance known. It is used in tools and saws, for engraving and cutting metals and glass; and in bits, for drilling through hard rock. A large diamond may be pierced with a tiny hole and used as a die through which metal can be drawn to make wire. Diamonds are found in a rare type of igneous rock called kimberlite (named for Kimberley, South Africa, where there are large mines). Other important sources are placer deposits along the coasts of southern Africa, and ancient stream placers in central Africa. Most of the world's production comes from the Republic of Zaire, the Republic of South Africa, Namibia, and the U.S.S.R. Synthetic diamond, in the form of fine grit, is manufactured in the United States and several other countries. (10)

DIATOMITE. A white, soft, porous sedimentary rock, made up of the tiny shells, or tests, of microscopic aquatic plants called diatoms. A single cubic inch of diatomite may contain as many as 40 million tests. Made of silica, these have extremely complex forms and thus a very large surface area. Diatomite powder—not fine enough to destroy the tests and test fragments—is used in filtering and clarifying wine, beer, syrup, and many other liquids, and as an ingredient of paint, plastics, and rubber. The country's largest deposit of diatomite is near Lompoc, Santa Barbara County, California. (19)

DIMENSION STONE. Rock that is cut, shaped, and sometimes polished, for use in building. Granite, marble, and limestone are widely used as dimension stone. (3)

DISSEMINATED DEPOSIT. A mineral deposit in which the ore mineral occurs as particles scattered through a large volume of rock. See also **PORPHYRY DEPOSIT.**

DOLOMITE. A sedimentary rock made up chiefly of the mineral of the same name, $CaMg(CO_3)_2$. Dolomite is used as a source of lime ($CaO \cdot MgO$), as a flux in steelmaking, as crushed stone and dimension stone, and in glassmaking. It is quarried on a large scale in Pennsylvania, Ohio, Indiana, Illinois, and Ontario.

DRILL PIPE. Steel pipe extending from the floor of a rotary drilling rig to the drill bit at the bottom of the hole. It turns the bit and conducts the drilling fluid downward from the surface. It is sometimes called the drill string.

DRILLING FLUID. In the rotary method of drilling for oil or gas, a fluid pumped down the drill pipe, through the bit, and back to the surface between the pipe and the walls of the hole. It removes rock cuttings, lubricates the bit, and plasters the walls of the hole. Water mixed with bentonite is a common drilling fluid. It is sometimes called drilling mud. (5,13)

DRY HOLE. A well drilled for oil or gas that produces neither. In spite of their name, dry holes generally produce hot salty or sulfurous water.

E

EIS. See **ENVIRONMENTAL IMPACT STATEMENT.**

ENVIRONMENTAL IMPACT. The effects of man's disturbance of the natural environment. The most urgent problems produced by mining involve use of the land surface. For example, at Bingham Canyon west of Salt Lake City, Utah, a whole mountain of low-grade copper ore has been removed. The site is now a big open pit that is still being mined. In central Florida, surface mining for phosphate rock affects large land areas; here, however, systematic reclamation of the surface is possible and produces useful land after mining. Disposal of mining wastes is a second major impact on the land. Water-borne mill tailings from operations like the one at Bingham Canyon are impounded behind dams in nearby canyons. The tailings sink and accumulate, and the water is re-used in the mill. Land in the Florida phosphate district must be set aside for storing waste slimes from the mills and waste gypsum from the refining plants. Some mining also has an effect on air and water quality, but these are generally closely controlled.

Other kinds of environmental problems are caused when a tanker loaded with crude oil breaks up and loses a part or all of its cargo, as happened in Prince William Sound, Alaska, in April 1989. Such spills not only pollute the water and foul the shoreline, but are also extremely damaging to all forms of marine life. Environmental clean-up, to the extent that it is possible, is a job for private, commercial, and governmental agencies. See also **PHOSPHOGYPSUM** and **SLIME.**

ENVIRONMENTAL IMPACT STATEMENT (EIS). A document prepared by industry or by a political agency on the environmental impact of proposals or actions that may significantly affect the quality of the human environment. Environmental impact statements are used as decision-making tools and are required by the National Environmental Policy Act of 1970.

EVAPORITES. Rocks and mineral deposits, such as salt, gypsum, potassium minerals, and borates, formed through the evaporation of a body of water.

EXPLORATION. 1. In the mining industry, the examination of a deposit after it has been found, with the object of appraising its size, shape, and value. Minor disturbance of the environment may be produced by access roads and drill-rig sites. 2. In the oil industry, drilling at a distance from known oil pools in the hope of finding a new pool. See also **WILDCAT WELL.**

F

FELDSPAR. A group of white, gray, and flesh-pink minerals, aluminum silicates with potassium, sodium, or calcium. The potassium and sodium varieties are used as a flux in making glass and ceramics. Much of the United States production of feldspar comes from the Spruce Pine district in the Blue Ridge Mountains of North Carolina, where the substance is obtained from a granitelike rock by froth flotation. See also **FROTH FLOTATION.**

FERROMANGANESE NODULES. Potato-shaped masses of mineral matter that litter large areas of the deep ocean floor. They consist largely of iron oxide and manganese oxide minerals, with small amounts of nickel, copper, and cobalt. Present interest is focused on sites in the eastern Pacific Ocean, between the latitudes of 9° N and 16° N, where the nodules are high in nickel and copper and very abundant. However, mining these nodules in the open ocean at depths from 2.5 to 3.75 miles (4 to 6 kilometers) poses technical problems of great complexity. Commercial mining is not likely to get under way for many years.

FIXED CARBON. The carbon in coal. In the standard analysis, fixed carbon is the material that remains after the removal of moisture, ash, and volatile matter.

FLINT CLAY. A nonplastic, highly refractory clay made chiefly of kaolinite.

FLUORSPAR. Commercial name for the mineral fluorite, which is calcium fluoride, CaF_2. Fluorspar is a colorless to yellow, green, blue, or purple mineral occurring typically as clusters of cubic crystals or as granular masses. (Rarely, crystalline masses of fluorite are found large enough for carving into vases and other objects made spectacular by the mineral's color.) Fluorspar is common in veins and replacement deposits in limestone, often accompanying galena and sphalerite, the ore minerals of lead and zinc. About 70 percent of fluorspar is used to make hydrofluoric acid, HF. Nearly half of the HF, in turn, goes into chlorofluorocarbons, the key ingredient in aerosol sprays. These chemicals are now believed to destroy ozone molecules in the upper atmosphere. An international agreement to freeze and later reduce consumption of chlorofluorocarbons was signed by twenty-four nations in Montreal in September 1987. The agreement went into effect in 1989. It will decrease the demand for fluorspar, but it is possible that fluorine-containing substitutes may be developed for the outlawed compounds. Fluorspar is also used in glass and enamels, and as a flux in steelmaking. United States production comes from mines in southern Illinois, but much fluorspar is imported, chiefly from Mexico.

FLUX. A substance that lowers the melting temperature of a mixture, increasing fluidity and saving heat energy. Examples are sodium carbonate in glassmaking, and fluorspar and limestone in steelmaking.

FRACTURING SAND. Clean quartz sand suspended in a fluid that is pumped rapidly under high pressure down the casing of an oil or gas well and into the reservoir rock. There the fluid enlarges existing openings and creates new fractures, allowing greater flow of oil or gas toward the well bore. The fluid is withdrawn, but the sand remains as a propping agent to keep the fractures open. Often termed frac sand.

FRASCH METHOD. A technique for obtaining elemental sulfur from subsurface deposits. It depends on the fact that sulfur melts at 110° C (230° F), not far above the boiling point of water. Wells are drilled into the sulfur-bearing rock, and water at about 163° C (325° F) is injected, melting the sulfur. Since sulfur is almost twice as heavy as water, the sulfur accumulates at the bottom of the well. It is raised to the surface through a pipe inside the water-injection casing, a lift being provided by compressed air introduced through a still smaller pipe within the sulfur line. The sulfur reaches the surface as a dark liquid, 99.5 percent pure. This is cooled to a bright yellow solid, or it may be piped into specially insulated rail cars or barges for shipment in liquid form. The production method was developed by Herman Frasch in 1895. (16)

FROTH FLOTATION. A technique for removing one mineral from other minerals with which it is intergrown in a rock. The rock is first pulverized into grains ranging in size from 0.04 to 0.004 inch (1 mm to 0.1 mm). This mill feed goes to a tank, where it is stirred up in water and a chemical is added. The chemical is one of several specialized organic compounds, which, experience has shown, will attach itself to the grains of the desired mineral (for example, feldspar), but will ignore the grains of the others (such as mica, quartz, and iron-bearing minerals). The chemical does this by giving each feldspar grain a water-repellent coating. In the next step, a flotation cell, the feed is agitated further and a frothing agent, such as pine oil or soap, is added. Shedding water, the feldspar grains cling to the soap bubbles and rise with them to form a froth at the top of the cell. This froth is mechanically skimmed off with paddles or simply overflows. It then enters a trough where the feldspar is washed and reclaimed by filtering. The other mineral grains, being readily wettable, do not attach themselves to the bubbles, and sink to the bottom of the cell. They may in turn form the feed for another flotation cycle whereby a different mineral is recovered.

Froth flotation is adaptable to a variety of ores, as for example in the separation of copper minerals from the rock in which they are found, of potassium-bearing minerals from associated salt, or of feldspar from granitic rock as described above. A large concentrating mill may have scores or hundreds of froth-flotation units. Such units form an effective disassembly line for taking rocks apart into their constituent minerals.

FULLER'S EARTH. A light-colored, nonplastic clay that is a natural bleaching agent—that is, it will remove coloring matter from substances with which it comes into contact. It is used in refining and decolorizing fats and oils.

G

GALLIUM (Ga). A metallic element used in the form of compounds, especially gallium arsenide. This is a component of semiconductors, light-emitting vacuum tubes, lasers, and other electronic devices for use in computers and satellites. Gallium occurs in very small amounts in many rocks and ores; most is produced as a byproduct in the treatment of bauxite for aluminum. The United States produces no gallium; France, West Germany, and Japan are the largest producers.

GANGUE. The part of an ore that is of no value but cannot be avoided in mining. It is separated from the ore mineral or minerals in a mill, and is disposed of as tailings.

GARNET. A group of six silicate minerals of several metals. The garnet of commerce is an iron-aluminum silicate, the dark reddish-brown variety called almandine. As this is a hard mineral, and breaks into angular grains, it makes a good abrasive. Garnet is used on sandpaper, and for finishing wood, leather, glass, and soft metals. A small amount of garnet is cut and polished as a semiprecious stone. A mineral of metamorphic rocks, garnet is mined in the Adirondack Mountains of New York and in northern Idaho.

GAS. See **NATURAL GAS.**

GEOPHONE. A sensitive electronic receiver designed to pick up vibrations transmitted through rock. Geophones are used in the seismic method of prospecting for oil. See also **SEISMIC PROSPECTING.**

GERMANIUM (Ge). A grayish white metallic element. This metal and its oxide are used in infrared optics, fiber optics, and semiconductors. Germanium occurs as a trace element in certain ores of lead and lead-zinc-copper. It also occurs in coal, and, if needed, could be obtained in large amounts from ash and flue dust at power plants.

GOLD. (Au, from the Latin *aurum*). A yellow metallic element with several remarkable properties. Gold has a specific gravity of 19.3, so is nearly twenty times as heavy as water. It is so soft and malleable that it can be beaten into thin sheets or drawn into fine wire. Gold does not react with most acids, and does not tarnish with time. It is nonmagnetic, and is an excellent conductor of heat and electricity. It is also regarded as the foremost precious metal. Large stocks of gold are held by governments in support of their currencies. The major commercial use is in jewelry and art objects; other uses are in electronic circuits and in dentistry.

Most of the world's gold comes from deposits in which the metal occurs as a separate mineral—that is, as native gold. In the famous Mother Lode district of California, it is closely intergrown with quartz in gold-quartz veins; some of the gold is in easily seen irregular fillings between quartz grains, but most is in fine specks barely visible to the unaided eye. In several major deposits in Nevada, native gold occurs in very fine particles in silicified limestone. In both these types of deposits, the gold seems to have come from hot hydrothermal solutions moving upward into the crust from deep bodies of magma. The gold is recovered by fine-grinding the ore and dissolving the gold in a cyanide solution, from which it is then precipitated.

An entirely different type of gold occurrence is the placer deposit. Here the gold occurs as loose grains, pea-size masses or—rarely!—large lumps or nuggets, in gravel deposits along stream channels. Placer discoveries started both the California Gold Rush of 1848 and the one to Alaska and the Yukon Territory in 1890. Anyone may pan for gold, by scooping up some promising gravel in a shallow pan, swirling it about in water, and allowing the lighter grains to overflow so that the heavy ones are concentrated at the bottom of the pan. Placer mining on a large scale is done by using strong jets of water, or by dredging. In the Republic of South Africa, the world's leading producer, gold occurs in what is apparently an ancient placer, now greatly altered and even changed into metamorphic rock. This fossil placer, in fact, is not loose gravel but solid rock and is found at depths as great as 12,000 feet (3,658 meters). A little of the world's gold is obtained as a byproduct in the processing of the ores of other metals, chiefly copper. Besides South Africa, the world's main producers of gold are the U.S.S.R., Canada, the United States, and Australia.

In the late 1980s the price of gold was about $400 per ounce. This meant that it was profitable to mine rock that contained only a fraction of an ounce per ton. A major producing company in Nevada was mining and processing gold ore in 1987 that averaged only 0.05 ounce (1.4 grams) per ton. The company was greatly encouraged when coring showed deeper ore with an average gold content of 0.93 ounce per ton, or nearly twenty times the content then being mined. Gold is by far the most actively sought among the metals. In 1986 more than forty new mines opened in the western United States; in 1987 thirteen new mines went into production in Canada.

Placer mining disturbs the stream course along which it is being done, washing down gravel banks and loading the stream with sediment. The problem is especially acute in Alaska, where water quality and fishing are important and there are many small placer mines. The U.S. Bureau of Mines has developed a water-treatment process and work is continuing. (8, 9)

GRANITE. An igneous rock consisting of visible interlocking grains of feldspar, quartz, and dark iron-magnesium minerals. Much granite is cut and polished for building stone and for monuments and memorials. Granite is also crushed for use as aggregate in concrete. There are large quarries in Vermont, North Carolina, and Georgia. Cutting, carving, or grinding granite may produce dust containing quartz (free silica). If breathed, this dust may produce silicosis, a lung disease. The dust may be removed by air suction or suppressed by keeping working surfaces wet.

GRAPHITE. A soft black mineral, a form of carbon (symbol: C). Graphite is so slippery that it is used as a lubricant; it is immune to very high temperatures, and so serves to line the molds into which molten metal is poured; it is such a good conductor of electricity that it is used in motors and dry-cell batteries. Minor uses are in paint and in lead pencils (which contain no lead). Graphite is a mineral of metamorphic rocks, where it occurs as flakes, scales, or bedded masses; it is all that is left of organic matter that was once in the parent rocks. Synthetic graphite is manufactured from a byproduct of oil refining. So-called graphite fibers, used in such products as tennis rackets and fishing rods, are not really graphite, but are carbon filaments manufactured from rayon or other carbon-bearing fibers. See also **COAL.** (2)

GRAVEL. A mixture of sand and pebbles or larger stream-worn rock fragments. It occurs in surface deposits formed by present or former streams. Removed from open pits and screened into size grades, gravel is used in large amounts as aggregate in concrete.

GROUNDWATER. Water that sinks into the ground. Moving downward under gravity, it may stay underground for long periods, but it will finally emerge as springs or seep into streams. Besides producing such spectacular features as Mammoth Cave and Carlsbad Caverns, groundwater is a prime resource for many cities and industries, and for farms needing irrigation. Most usable groundwater comes from within a few hundred feet of the surface; deeper waters are so heavily loaded with dissolved mineral matter that they are no value except rarely as brines. In some regions, as in parts of southwestern United States, more groundwater is taken from wells than enters the water-bearing rocks naturally. Such mining of groundwater has severely lowered the water table, or upper surface of water-saturated rocks, and will eventually place a limit on groundwater pumping. In some places, as in the Santa Clara Valley, California, reservoirs have been built to catch rainfall and snowmelt and allow it to sink in and replenish the groundwater.

Groundwater may be contaminated by phosphate or nitrate fertilizers carried downward in solution from farmers' fields, as well as from municipal and industrial wastes. Some wastes generated at metal refineries may contain traces of lead and other metals that are harmful to humans. These waters are monitored by the Environmental Protection Agency and by state and local authorities.

GYPSUM. A white to gray sedimentary rock, made up chiefly of the mineral of the same name. This is hydrous calcium sulfate, $CaSO_4 \cdot 2H_2O$. Rock gypsum is compact and finely crystalline, and occurs in beds ranging in thickness from three or four feet (0.9 or 1.2 meters) to more than 100 feet (30 meters). Gypsum is the raw material of plaster, as used in wallboard and other building materials. It is a common rock, mined in nineteen states and many foreign countries. Gypsum is an evaporite, formed when ancient sea waters dried up. (3)

H

HAFNIUM (Hf). A metallic element occurring along with zirconium in the mineral zircon. Hafnium is used in nuclear reactors, in high-temperature refractories, and in hafnium-niobium carbide for tools used in drilling and cutting.

HALITE. A white to gray nonmetallic mineral, chemical name sodium chloride (NaCl). Halite is essentially the only mineral of rock salt. It also occurs with other evaporites, especially potassium minerals and sodium minerals. See also **ROCK SALT.**

HARDROCK MINING. An informal term for the underground mining of metallic ore deposits.

HEAVY MINERALS. Dark sand grains with a high specific gravity. Heavy minerals of value include magnetite (specific gravity 5.17), a source of iron; monazite (5.0) and xenotime (4.5), rare-earth minerals; zircon (4.7), the ore mineral of zirconium; and the two titanium minerals, ilmenite (4.5) and rutile (4.2). Heavy minerals are mined in placer deposits. They may readily be separated from quartz and from each other by gravity methods. See also **PLACER.**

HELIUM (He). An element occurring as a light inert colorless gas down to -270° C (-454° F). It is used wherever very low temperatures are required, as in refrigerating and in the testing of superconducting materials. Helium is also used in arc welding, in growing transistor crystals, in deep-sea diving equipment, and as a lifting gas for blimps and balloons. Helium is a component of certain natural gases found in the United States, especially in Kansas, Utah, and Texas.

HIGH-SULFUR COAL. Bituminous coal that contains more than 1 percent sulfur. On burning, such coal yields gaseous sulfur dioxide (SO_2), which combines with atmospheric moisture to form sulfuric acid (H_2SO_4), an ingredient of acid rain. Intensive research efforts are under way to find methods of removing sulfur from coal before the coal is burned. Free sulfur, along with pyrite (iron sulfide), can be removed by crushing and cleaning, but the sulfur locked into the organic matter can be removed only by first converting the coal to gas or liquid, a costly process. See also **DESULFURIZATION.**

HOST ROCK. The body of rock that contains a mineral deposit. Thus granite might be the host rock of gold-quartz veins, or limestone the host rock of a replacement deposit of fluorspar.

HYDROCARBON. A compound containing only hydrogen and carbon. Examples are methane, CH_4, and benzene, C_6H_6. Most hydrocarbons are much more complex than these.

HYDROTHERMAL SOLUTIONS. Hot waters in the earth's crust. Many mineral deposits have been formed by precipitation from such solutions. Most hydrothermal solutions are of igneous origin, but the source of others is not clear. See also **BLACK SMOKER** and **WHITE SMOKER.**

I

INDIUM (In). A rare metallic element occurring in small amounts in zinc ores. Indium is used in electrical and electronic components, and in solders, alloys, and coatings.

INDUSTRIAL MINERALS. All those solid substances that man extracts from the earth except metals, fuels, and gems. Industrial minerals are the raw materials of the ceramic, chemical, construction, fertilizer, glassmaking, and refractories industries, among others. Since the group includes rocks as well as minerals, a more descriptive term would be industrial rocks and minerals. An informal synonym is nonmetallics. (2, 5)

IODINE (I). A nonmetallic element. In its solid form iodine consists of grayish black crystals that readily vaporize to a violet-colored gas. Iodine is used in animal feeds, especially for beef cattle; in inks and dyes; in photography; and in antiseptics. It is obtained from brines associated with natural gas, especially in Japan. Some iodine is also produced as a byproduct of nitrate mining in Chile. A Japanese company produces forty tons of iodine per month from well brines in Oklahoma.

IRON (**Fe**, from the Latin *ferrum*). A metallic element that is the fourth most abundant element in the earth's crust. Iron can be worked into different shapes, rusts readily in moist air, and is the most common and important of the metals. It is used alone, as cast iron or wrought iron, but is far more important as the main ingredient of steel. Steel is an alloy of iron with a small amount of carbon and generally with one or more other metals, such as chromium, nickel, cobalt, or molybdenum.

The most important ore minerals of iron are two oxides that commonly occur together. These are hematite, a dark red mineral, Fe_2O_3, and magnetite, a gray to black mineral, Fe_3O_4. These minerals have a theoretical iron content of 70 percent and 72.4 percent respectively, but the actual content is considerably lower because of silica and other impurities. Enormous deposits of deep red hematite-magnetite ore were discovered in the Lake Superior region of Minnesota in the latter half of the last century. These deposits have furnished 78 percent of the iron consumed by the United States. Two-thirds of that total came from a single district called the Mesabi Range, where the ore was mined in tremendous open pits. The average iron content of the Mesabi ores was 56.8 percent. By the 1950s, however, the rich ores of the Lake Superior region had been largely exhausted. Attention since that time has focused on lower-grade siliceous ore called taconite. Large bodies of rich hematite-magnetite ore are known in Labrador, Australia, the U.S.S.R., and Brazil. The world supply of iron ore exceeds the demand. See also **TACONITE.** (8, 11)

K

KAOLIN. A soft white clay consisting chiefly of the mineral kaolinite, a hydrous aluminum silicate. Kaolin is used as a filler in paper and other products, in ceramic whiteware, and in refractories. It is dug from sedimentary deposits on the coastal plain of South Carolina and Georgia. In Cornwall, England, kaolin is washed by hydraulic jets from masses of decomposed granite. Processing includes washing and filtering to remove quartz grains, high-intensity magnetic separation to remove even slight traces of iron-bearing minerals, and extremely fine grinding. (2, 5)

KEROGEN. Fossilized organic matter, mostly the remains of algae and algal plant cells (spores and pollen). It is found in oil shale. See also **OIL SHALE.**

KYANITE. A mineral, chemical name aluminum silicate (Al_2SiO_5). A blue or light green mineral, it occurs in long, thin-bladed crystals or crystal aggregates in metamorphic rocks. Together with two related minerals, kyanite is a premium refractory mineral, used in the steel, glass, and ceramics industries. There is one mine in the United States, in Virginia. The Republic of South Africa is a major producer of kyanite.

L

LAND SUBSIDENCE. Lowering of the ground surface owing to the removal of earth materials from below. It may result from the removal of oil from wells, as at Long Beach, California, or from the withdrawal of groundwater. At Santa Clara, California, the land surface has subsided as much as eight feet (2.4 meters) owing to removal of groundwater. Such subsidence is slow and gradual. Local subsidence, damaging to houses and roadways, may occur above underground coal mines, as at places in western Pennsylvania and eastern Ohio. Longwall mining is especially prone to cause such subsidence. See also **LONGWALL MINING.**

LEAD (Pb, from Latin *plumbum*). A heavy gray metallic element. About 70 percent is used in automobile batteries and gasoline additives. Other uses are in ammunition, glass, paint, type metal, and tubes or containers. Most of the United States production comes from mines in Missouri. The chief ore mineral of lead is galena, PbS. This sulfide, along with sphalerite, the sulfide of zinc, occurs in vein and replacement deposits in limestone.

Lead is toxic in air or water. Its use in gasoline is due to be phased out by 1992 if not earlier. A once-common paint pigment, white lead or lead carbonate, has now been almost entirely replaced by titanium dioxide. The Environmental Protection Agency is expected to lower its permissible standard for lead in water from 50 to 20 parts per billion.

LIGHTWEIGHT AGGREGATE. Aggregate that weighs less than ordinary sand, gravel, or crushed stone. It includes pumice, expanded perlite, expanded vermiculite, expanded or bloated shale, and porous slag. Used chiefly in concrete blocks and interior plasters, lightweight aggregate provides good insulation against heat and sound, is easier than ordinary aggregate to lift and handle, and decreases the dead weight of structures in which it is used.

LIGNITE. A brownish-black coal, intermediate between peat and bituminous coal in the coal development series. Beds of lignite are geologically young, and are typically flat-lying at or near the surface. The texture of the original woody material can often still be seen. The United States has large deposits of lignite, especially in eastern Montana, but lignite is relatively unimportant as a fuel in this country because we have so much of the more valuable bituminous coal. Lignite is much used in central Europe, where coal is in short supply. A synonym is brown coal. See also **COAL.**

LIME. Known also by its chemical name, calcium oxide (CaO). It is sometimes referred to as quicklime. Lime is produced in the form of white porous lumps by calcining limestone to drive off the carbon dioxide (CO_2) from the calcite ($CaCO_3$) of the limestone. Quicklime tends to reabsorb carbon dioxide, and also to combine with water, so that much CaO is processed into a stable form, hydrated lime $Ca(OH)_2$. Lime is essential in many industrial fields. In steelmaking, it combines with silica, alumina, sulfur, and phosphorus to make a silicate slag, which is drawn off. Lime helps to soften drinking water for municipal systems, and is used in treating industrial liquid wastes.

66

It helps to neutralize acid mine drainage. It is a key substance in the manufacture of kraft paper (brown paper, shopping bags, etc.) and in the refining of beet sugar. Lime is one of the three main constituents of glass. It is used in the scrubbers that remove sulfur dioxide (SO_2) from smokestack gases at coal-fired power plants. It stabilizes claylike, plastic soil, so that it will support roads or buildings. Together with salt, sulfur, and coal or petroleum, lime is a mainstay of the chemical industry. In 1986, lime producers at 115 plants in thirty-five states produced 14 million tons of lime, valued at $724 million.

LIMESTONE. A sedimentary rock of which at least 50 percent is the mineral calcite (calcium carbonate, $CaCO_3$). Impurities include dolomite, chert, and clay. Limestone with more than 95 percent $CaCO_3$ is known in commerce as high-calcium stone. Most limestone originated as a layer of shells, shell fragments, and limy mud on the floor of an ancient sea. Shells preserved as fossils are common in some limestone layers. Limestone may be dense and fine-grained, granular like sugar, or coarse-grained, with calcite crystals up to one-fourth inch in diameter. Organic matter may make the rock dark gray or even black, but the most common colors range from light gray to tan. Some limestones are thin-bedded and slabby, others are in layers a foot or two thick, and a few are in massive uniform beds.

Limestone is the most versatile and widely used rock in the earth's crust. About 68 percent of the total is crushed for concrete aggregate. The rock's structure of interlocking calcite grains makes the fragments strong and gives them a high resistance to freezing and thawing. Limestone produces no quartz dust to scar workmen's lungs or abrade machinery. Deposits of limestone are widely distributed. For these reasons, some 500 million tons of limestone is used for aggregate every year—more than twice as much as all other rock types combined. The market is the seemingly endless demand for concrete. As if this weren't enough, limestone is used in construction in another form: dimension stone. Blocks may be cut, carved, and/or polished for use on outside walls or interior panels and floors. Many public buildings in the eastern and central United States are faced with a light gray or buff limestone quarried in southern Indiana. The East Building of the National Gallery of Art, in Washington, D.C., has inside and outside walls of a pinkish gray coarse-grained limestone from Tennessee. Such uses of limestone are visible and attractive but they account for only a tiny fraction of the country's total limestone tonnage.

Other uses of limestone depend on the chemistry of $CaCO_3$ rather than on the physical properties of the rock. Limestone is the source of lime, and the chief raw material of cement. The rock may be finely ground and spread on cropland as a fertilizer and soil conditioner. Limestone of high purity is pulverized into a white powder and used in paint, plastics, and other products. Limestone also goes into the smelter with iron ore, acting as a flux to combine with impurities and form slag.

Limestone—crushed, powdered, cut, or calcined—is the preeminent example of a useful earth material. In our complex industrial society, life without limestone would be quite impossible.

LITHIUM (Li). A soft silver-white metallic element that is the lightest known metal. Lithium carbonate is used in the production of aluminum, and the carbonate and other compounds are important in a wide variety of products. These include glass and ceramics, greases, batteries, medicine, and solar-energy units. Aluminum-lithium alloys appeared on the market in 1987, and most aircraft manufacturers stated plans to use them in their newly designed airliners. Commercial production in the United States comes mainly from the Kings Mountain district of North Carolina, where the mineral spodumene, a grayish green lithium silicate, occurs in pegmatites. Other lithium-rich pegmatites are mined in Zimbabwe and Namibia in southern Africa.

Brines from beneath a dry lake bed in Clayton Valley, Nevada, yield lithium at an evaporating plant. The largest known concentration of lithium is in the brines of a dry lake in the Atacama Desert of Chile.

LODE. 1. A mineral deposit consisting of a zone or series of veins. 2. A mineral deposit in solid rock, as contrasted with a placer deposit.

LOG. See **WELL LOG.**

LONGWALL MINING. A method of underground mining in flat-lying beds, especially of coal. Temporary support at a long working face is supplied by timbers; the roof caves in as mining progresses. The process is highly automated. Almost all the coal is removed, in contrast to the room-and-pillar method. See also **ROOM-AND-PILLAR MINING.**

LOW-GRADE DEPOSIT. An ore deposit having a very low concentration of the desired metal. Mining involves moving and processing enormous amounts of rock, more than 95 percent of which must be disposed of as waste. Most the world's copper comes from low-grade deposits. See also **PORPHYRY DEPOSIT.**

M

MAGNESIA. Known also by its chemical name, magnesium oxide (MgO). Magnesia is a white, dense, inert compound. It has a very high melting point and is used as a refractory in steel furnaces, cement kilns, and similar equipment. Magnesia is produced by calcining the mineral magnesite; the refractory grade, known as dead-burned magnesia, is formed at 1,450°–1,750° C (2,640°–3,180° F). Other sources of magnesia are dolomite, well brines, and seawater. About one-quarter of the magnesia produced is used in animal feeds, special cements, and magnesium chemicals, including the well-known milk of magnesia.

MAGNESITE. A white to gray nonmetallic mineral, chemical name magnesium carbonate ($MgCO_3$). Magnesite is the main source of magnesia. Magnesite occurs as replacement bodies in dolomite and as alteration products of magnesium-rich metamorphic rocks such as serpentine. A dozen countries produce magnesite. The only commercial deposit in the United States is at Gabbs, Nevada, about 140 miles (225 kilometers) southeast of Reno.

MAGNESIUM (Mg). A silver-white metallic element. It burns with a brilliant white light and is used in photographic flash bulbs. Magnesium is an important alloying metal with aluminum. See also **MAGNESIA** and **MAGNESITE.**

MANGANESE (Mn). A grayish white metallic element that rusts like iron but is not magnetic. About 95 percent is used as an alloy in steel; manganese is the fourth most widely used metal (after iron, aluminum, and copper). But the remaining five percent is also important. According to one authority, manganese is used in feed, food, fertilizer, fungicides, facebricks, frits, flux, fragrances, flavors, foundries, and ferrites, as well as fluorescent tubes and fine chemicals! The chief ore mineral of manganese is pyrolusite, a heavy iron-gray oxide, MnO_2, most of which is found in sedimentary deposits. Manganese is produced in more than thirty countries; by far the largest producers are the U.S.S.R. and South Africa. See also **FERROMANGANESE NODULES.**

MARBLE. A metamorphic rock consisting almost entirely of tightly intergrown crystals of the mineral calcite. Pure marble is brilliant white. Shades or streaks of gray are produced by graphite; of pink and yellow, by a little iron oxide. Its crystalline texture allows marble to take a polish. The stone is widely used in public buildings, memorials, and statues. Pure marble is also a source of finely ground calcium carbonate, used as a filler in paint and plastics. There are famous deposits of marble in Greece and Italy. In the United States, marble is quarried chiefly in Vermont, Georgia, Alabama, and Colorado.

MERCURY (**Hg,** from the Greek *hydrargyros*, flowing silver). A heavy silver-white metallic element. Mercury is a liquid at ordinary temperatures; a synonym is quicksilver. The metal is used in thermometers and electrical switches, and is alloyed with silver in amalgam for dental fillings. Mercury compounds have numerous uses in the chemical industries, and in the prevention of mildew in plants and seeds. The chief ore mineral of mercury is cinnabar, HgS, a bright red mineral that occurs as veins and replacement bodies. The major sources are Spain and Italy. Mercury is poisonous if inhaled as vapor or ingested with food.

METAL. A chemical element that can be stretched, drawn, or hammered without breaking, and that is a good conductor of heat and electricity. A few metals, for example gold, occur in the earth's crust as native elements, but most occur as compounds with oxygen, sulfur, or other nonmetallic elements. Examples are manganese in MnO_2 (pyrolusite), and copper and iron in $CuFeS_2$ (chalcopyrite).

MICA (from the Latin *micare*, to shine or sparkle). A group of hydrous aluminum silicate minerals with such well developed cleavage that they can be split into thin flexible sheets. The main mica of commerce is muscovite, or white mica. Sheets of muscovite, rarely more than 2 or 3 inches (5 or 7.6 centimeters) in diameter, are resistant to electrical current and are used as nonconducting elements in such familiar appliances as toasters. Sheet mica is obtained from pegmatites, mainly in India; much hand labor is involved. Far more important in industry is ground mica, recovered as a byproduct in the milling of rock for feldspar or of clay for kaolin. Dry grinding produces rough-edged mica particles that are used in plasterboard joint cement, as a dusting agent to keep roll roofing from sticking, and in oil-well drilling. Wet grinding produces a powder of thin flat platelets that glitter and are used in paint and rubber and on wall paper. The United States is a major producer of ground mica; more than 60 percent of the output is a byproduct of the milling of feldspar in the Spruce Pine district of North Carolina. See also **FROTH FLOTATION.**

MINE. An excavation, generally underground, from which a valuable earth material is extracted. The term has also been used for an operation by which sulfur is obtained from wells. See also **OPEN PIT, QUARRY,** and **STRIP MINE.**

MINERAL DEPOSIT. See **ORE DEPOSIT.**

MINERAL RESOURCES. See **RESOURCES.**

MINERAL RIGHTS. Ownership of all mineral deposits that may be present in a given tract of land, together with the right to explore and to mine if a discovery is made. In selling some lands to private owners, the federal government and several states sell the surface rights only, as for farming or grazing. The mineral rights remain with the original owner.

MINERAL WOOL. Fibers made by blowing or spinning threads of molten rock, slag, or glass. Mats of this material are used for thermal insulation. Fine dust from mineral wool may be injurious to the lungs or irritating to the skin. Synonyms: rock wool, fiberglass.

MINING. A general term for the extraction of solid earth materials. It may refer to underground operations or to surface works such as pits and quarries. Extraction of sulfur via wells is sometimes termed mining. See also **SOLUTION MINING.**

MINING DISTRICT. An informal term for an area where one or more mines are situated.

MOLYBDENUM (Mo). A soft metallic element used chiefly as an alloy of iron and steel. A superalloy containing molybdenum is used in jet engines. Molybdic oxide, MoO_3, is used in oil refining. The principal ore mineral is molybdenite, MoS_2, which is found in large low-grade porphyry deposits. Colorado is a major producer.

N

NATURAL GAS. Petroleum vapor as it comes from the well. Its main constituent is methane, CH_4. Natural gas may occur alone, or it may be dissolved in crude oil, from which it is separated at the surface. Impurities, such as hydrogen sulfide, must be removed before the gas can be put into the pipeline for commercial or domestic use.

NEPHELINE SYENITE. An igneous rock resembling granite but containing no quartz. It is made up chiefly of feldspar and the mineral nepheline, a silicate with a composition similar to that of feldspar. These minerals give nepheline syenite a high content of alumina, making it an important raw material of glass and ceramics. Most nepheline syenite contains dark iron-rich minerals and cannot be used; the only commercially important deposit in North America is at Blue Mountain, Ontario, about midway between Toronto and Ottawa.

NICKEL (Ni). A hard metallic element that is highly resistant to corrosion. It is used chiefly in stainless steel and as a film or coating in such products as automobile parts, kitchen utensils, and boating equipment. The chief nickel ore mineral is pentlandite, an iron-nickel sulfide, $(Fe, Ni)_9S_8$. Pentlandite is mined on a large scale at Sudbury, Ontario. The United States produces no nickel.

NIOBIUM (Nb). A gray metallic element that is used as an alloying material in the steel and aerospace industries. Niobium was formerly called columbium, and its steel alloys are still known as ferrocolumbium. The United States produces no niobium; Brazil and Canada are the major producers.

NITRATES. A general term for earth materials rich in nitrogen, commonly in the form of sodium nitrate, $NaNO_3$. This compound, along with common salt and other saline minerals, is mined from sandy and clayey surface deposits at places in the Atacama Desert of Chile. Sodium nitrate is used as fertilizer. Although reserves are large the deposits are now of minor importance, because most of the nitrogen for fertilizer is produced synthetically in the form of ammonia, NH_3, the nitrogen coming from the atmosphere and the hydrogen from natural gas. Heavy application of nitrate fertilizers to croplands may put undesirable amounts of nitrogen into surface or underground waters. Nitrates absorbed from drinking water reduce the oxygen-carrying capacity of the blood, a problem that may affect infants. Nitrogen and phosphorus in surface waters may cause tiny algae to bloom, or grow very rapidly, reducing the area of open water and using up the oxygen needed by fish and other water-dwellers.

NONMETALLICS. Industrial minerals.

O

OFFSHORE DEPOSIT. 1. An oil or gas pool below the sea floor. 2. A deposit of sand and gravel on the sea floor, close to the land and under less than 200 feet (61 meters) of water. Such deposits are worked by dredging in Britain and Japan, where onshore deposits have been depleted. Large gravel deposits are known off the New Jersey and Massachusetts coasts, and it is likely that they will soon be exploited.

OFFSHORE DRILLING. Drilling wells for oil and gas in such areas as the Gulf of Mexico, the Arabian Gulf, and the North Sea. Water depths of several hundred feet are not uncommon. Drilling rigs that stand on the sea floor are among the tallest structures ever made. Offshore drilling is dangerous work for the crews on the rigs and is a potential source of oil spills and other pollution. Nevertheless, much oil and gas are produced from such drilling. (13)

OIL. See **CRUDE OIL.**

OIL FIELD. A general term for a group of closely related oil pools.

OIL POOL. An underground accumulation of petroleum that will yield oil in economic quantities. It is not a pool in the ordinary sense; the oil is held in the pore spaces of porous rock. An oil pool can be compared to a saturated sponge.

Except for a thin zone just beneath the surface, the rocks below ground are saturated with water. In some regions underlain by thick deposits of sedimentary rock, a second fluid is present in the subsurface: crude oil (generally with some gas in solution). As crude oil is lighter than water, it tends to move upward through the water-saturated rocks, following porous and permeable rock layers toward the surface. More often than not, however, the oil encounters some sort of obstruction—known as a trap—that halts its upward migration. The oil accumulates, displacing the water and forming a pool. Traps are of many kinds. If the rocks are in a gentle arch or fold, the oil may accumulate at the top under an impermeable roof rock, like balloons in a domed stadium. A trap may be produced where the reservoir rock ends against a fault. Or the layer containing the oil may simply become less and less porous and permeable in the upward direction, until at length the oil can no longer move and backs up, like people crowding into a dead-end street. Ancient coral reefs, now forming masses of porous limestone deep belowground, may contain big oil pools. Many traps are produced by the upward movement of salt.

A common reservoir rock is sandstone that is weakly cemented, so that many of the pore spaces between the sand grains are open. Furthermore, these open pores are connected, so that the rock is highly permeable. Other common reservoir rocks are limestone and dolomite. In such carbonate rocks water has often produced solution cavities—ranging in size from a pinhead to a cavern—in which oil may accumulate. However the reservoir is formed, if enough gas is present the oil will flow naturally from a well owing to the release of gas pressure. It may also flow because of water pressure in the reservoir rock. Wells have to be pumped after an initial period of free flow. Gushers—flowing wells that are out of control—are spectacular but disastrous. They wreck the drilling rig, waste oil and reservoir pressure, foul up the surrounding area, and, worst of all, may catch fire. They are avoided by placing a heavy blowout preventer on the well casing, and by using weighted drilling mud.

Since oil pools are entirely underground, they cannot be found by a prospector with a hammer. They must be located by a combination of regional geology, geophysical study, and information from previously drilled wells, if any, in the area of interest. With these aids, all the petroleum geologist can do is to place a wildcat well where he hopes a pool is present. The actual discovery of the oil pool is done by the bit as it bores its way downward through the rocks. See also **BARITE, BENTONITE, SALT DOMES,** and **WELL LOG.** (13)

OIL SAND. 1. An informal synonym for reservoir rock. 2. Sand containing dark viscous oil, exposed at the surface. Oil sands of this type in Alberta, Canada, contain the world's largest known deposit of oil, some 600 billion barrels. The deposit is being mined on a modest scale, but the cold climate and other factors make the sand expensive to mine and refine. See also **RESERVOIR ROCK.**

OIL SHALE. An unfortunate name for a rock that is not shale and does not contain oil. Oil shale is a brown or black finely laminated sedimentary rock containing organic matter in the form of kerogen. On being crushed and heated in a closed retort, the rock can be distilled to yield oil. Large deposits of oil shale are known in western Colorado, but they are not economical to mine. Not only is much energy needed to distill the shale, but the process requires large amounts of water, which is not readily available in the region. Environmental problems arise in connection with the disposal of spent shale—which, oddly enough, takes up more space after the organic matter has been removed than it does in its natural form. No one wants to fill canyons with spent shale. Oil shale remains a potential resource for the future. See also **KEROGEN.**

OIL-WATER CONTACT. The lower boundary of an oil pool. The oil-water contact is the surface above which the reservoir rock contains oil and below which the rock is saturated with water.

OLIVINE. A gray-green mineral that is a silicate of magnesium and iron: $(Mg,Fe)_2SiO_4$. It is used in the blast furnace, where its magnesium and silica act as fluxing agents and slag conditioners. It is also used in refractory bricks, as its melting point is about $1,800°$ C ($3,270°$ F). Olivine is a mineral of igneous rocks, and in a few rocks it is essentially the only mineral present. It is mined at Twin Sisters Mountain, about 20 miles (32 kilometers) east of Bellingham, Washington, and in North Carolina about 35 miles (56 kilometers) southwest of Asheville. The world's largest producer of olivine is Norway.

OPEN PIT. A surface excavation from which sand, gravel, clay, or other unconsolidated materials are extracted. See also **QUARRY** and **STRIP MINE.**

ORE. Any naturally occurring material from which one or more valuable minerals may be profitably extracted. The term is often modified by the name of the desired mineral, as in fluorspar ore, or by the name of the metal obtained after processing, as in copper ore. The term ore has an economic meaning as well as a geologic one: a body of rock containing a little gold may be worthless today, but it may become ore tomorrow if the price of gold increases enough to make mining profitable. See also **GANGUE.**

ORE DEPOSIT. A localized body of ore. The term refers to rock that contains a valuable ore mineral plus worthless rock, or gangue, that must be handled in order to obtain the ore mineral. Some ore deposits are no more than a few feet thick and a few hundred feet long; others are the size of a mountain. Some are very rich, others low-grade. Some ore deposits can be worked on a small scale, others require a very large investment.

Ore deposits are of many origins. Bauxite, the rock from which aluminum is extracted, is found in widespread near-surface deposits. It is the result of intense weathering of aluminum-rich rocks in a tropical climate. Pyrolusite, the main ore mineral of manganese, formed as sedimentary accumulations in shales and limestones. The immense chromite deposits of southern Africa are in layers of igneous origin. As a body of magma crystallized, early-formed crystals settled to the bottom of the magma chamber, and chromite was concentrated in layers up to a few feet thick. Many ore deposits were formed in preexisting rocks by hydrothermal solutions derived from masses of cooling magma. Such is the origin of the immense porphyry-copper deposits in geologically young mountain chains like the Rockies and the Andes. Many deposits of galena and sphalerite, the ore minerals of lead and zinc, show evidence of having been deposited by hydrothermal solutions. These deposits are commonly in flat-lying limestone beds, where the galena and sphalerite occur in veins and replacement bodies. Ore deposits of fluorspar are also of this type.

An altogether different type of deposit is the placer. The lower levels of certain stream gravels and beach sands contain concentrations of minerals that are hard, inert, heavy, or otherwise immune to being ground up in nature's mill and washed away. Beach sands yield diamonds in southern Africa and titanium minerals in Western Australia. Stream placers in Indonesia and Malaysia yield cassiterite, the ore mineral of tin. Among the richest known gold deposits are those of South Africa, which are apparently in a fossil placer now hardened into rock and deeply buried. There is good evidence that some ore deposits whose origin has long been questioned were formed on the floors of ancient seas by jets of mineral-laden hydrothermal solutions pouring out of vents into the sea water. Some deposits of lead, zinc, copper, and barite are apparently of this origin.

Ore deposits as a group have two features in common. The first is irregular or scattered distribution. Ore deposits are not arranged for the convenience of mankind; gold, as they say, is where you find it. Many deposits are far from markets, and millions of dollars must be spent on getting supplies and equipment in, and ore concentrates out. If the mine is in scenic or recreational country, environmental problems must be solved. The second feature is exhaustibility. No ore deposit lasts forever. Sooner or later the deposit will be worked out, and the entire operation will have to close down. Naturally, the management of the mine will want to put this day off for as long as possible. So the company's geologists will be asked to find an extension of the deposit, or to locate another deposit—preferably close by. The company's engineers, meanwhile, will try to devise a way of treating lower-grade ore, and so greatly enlarge the mine's reserves. Matters like these are on the mind of management as it tries to answer the biggest question at any ore deposit: How many years' supply of ore do we have left? See also **BLACK SMOKER** and **WHITE SMOKER.**

ORE MINERAL. The mineral of value in an ore, as chalcopyrite in copper ore. The ore mineral must be separated from associated gangue and then processed to yield the desired metal.

OVERBURDEN. Soil, subsoil, and rock that must be removed before a mineral deposit can be extracted in a quarry, open pit, or strip mine. Overburden at most operations was once cast aside and left in unsightly heaps, but since the 1960s environmental pressures have imposed better housekeeping: most operators now put the overburden in temporary piles; then, when mining has been completed, they spread it over the area, restoring the land surface to a useful and attractive form.

P

PEAT. An unconsolidated deposit of partly decayed plant remains, spongy when wet and porous when dry. Peat accumulates in a bog or swamp, as dead plant matter falls into acidic water and is preserved. Leaves, bark, and woody fragments can be plainly seen. Peat is the first stage in the geologic evolution of coal. Plant nurseries and home gardeners use peat as a potting material and soil conditioner. See also **COAL.**

PEGMATITE. An igneous rock, generally of granitic composition and very large grain size, pegmatite is sometimes called giant granite. Crystals several inches or a couple of feet across are common in many pegmatites; exceptionally, crystals of feldspar, quartz, or mica are found that are several feet across and weigh a ton or more. Most pegmatites are sheetlike or disklike in form; others occur as pipes, pods, or scoop-shaped bodies. They occur in metamorphic and igneous rocks. Pegmatites have been mined for feldspar and sheet mica, and at a few places for topaz and other rare minerals. Such mining is well described as gopher-hole work, and is costly because of the hand labor required. Pegmatites in the Kings Mountain district, North Carolina, are rich in spodumene, a lithium mineral, and can be mined in bulk by means of mechanical equipment.

PERLITE. A white to gray igneous rock that is a natural glass. Two to five percent of perlite is combined water. When grains of crushed perlite are rapidly heated, their water is converted to steam and the grains swell or pop like popcorn. Expanded perlite is used as lightweight aggregate in plaster, wallboard, and concrete; as a filtering medium for liquids; and as a rooting and soil-conditioning agent in potting plants. More than 85 percent of the United States production of perlite comes from a cluster of volcanic hills in north-central New Mexico, aptly known as No Agua (No Water) Peaks. Crushed and screened perlite is shaped in crude forms and expanded at plants near major markets. (2)

PETROLEUM. A general term for highly complex mixtures of hydrogen and carbon, including crude oil, natural gas, and natural asphalt. Common impurities are nitrogen, oxygen, and sulfur. Sometimes the term petroleum is used to refer only to crude oil. (13)

PHOSPHATE ROCK. Any rock that contains enough of the mineral apatite to be of value as a source of phosphorus or phosphatic compounds. About 90 percent of world production is sedimentary phosphate rock, or phosphorite. Major United States production comes from loose gravelly deposits in central Florida and on the coast of North Carolina, and from deposits of sedimentary rock in Idaho and adjacent Wyoming and Utah. Phosphate rock is the raw material of phosphoric acid, the parent of phosphate fertilizers. An important by-product of the Florida manufacturing plants is fluorine. Unwanted wastes include slime and phosphogypsum. See also **PHOS-PHOGYPSUM** and **SLIME.**

PHOSPHOGYPSUM. Impure gypsum produced as waste in the manufacture of phosphate fertilizer in central Florida. It has no industrial uses and must be stored in large piles, or gyp stacks, that are unsightly and use up valuable land.

PHOSPHORITE. Sedimentary phosphate rock, generally of marine origin. Its phosphate-bearing mineral, apatite, is in the form of microcrystalline pellets and nodules, and also as fragments of shell and bone.

PLACER. A deposit of sand or gravel that contains particles of a valuable mineral. For example, gold has been mined from stream placers in Alaska and the Yukon Territory, and ilmenite and other heavy minerals from beach placers along the coast of Western Australia. The word placer is of Spanish origin and is pronounced *plasser*.

PLATINUM (Pt). A gray metallic element that is highly resistant to corrosion. Its greatest use is in automobile catalytic converters, where it helps reduce air pollution from the exhaust system. Other uses are in petroleum refining, jewelry, and dental alloys. Platinum is a precious metal and sells for $450 to $650 per ounce. The United States depends almost entirely on imports; the main producer is the Republic of South Africa. A mine in Montana, opened in early 1987, may change this picture.

PORPHYRY DEPOSIT. A large body of fine-grained igneous rock containing scattered large crystals, generally of feldspar, and small grains of chalcopyrite and other copper-sulfide minerals. The porphyry is the ore; it is of low grade, averaging less than one percent copper. What porphyry deposits lack in richness they make up for in size: they may be a mile or more in length and width and many hundreds of feet thick. The rock is mined in bulk in large open pits.

Other metals besides copper found in porphyry deposits are molybdenum and tin. (11)

POTASH. An informal term for minerals, compounds, or processed products containing potassium. See also **POTASSIUM MINERALS.**

POTASSIUM MINERALS. Several sedimentary evaporite minerals that are rich in the element potassium (symbol: K, from the Latin *kalium*). The chief commercial mineral among these is sylvite (potassium chloride, KCl); other potassium chlorides and sulfates have local importance. As potassium is one of the three primary plant foods (with nitrogen and phosphorus), nearly all the production of potassium minerals goes into fertilizer. Sylvite and its relatives occur in sedimentary beds, commonly accompanied by beds of halite (common salt, sodium chloride, NaCl). Like salt, the potassium minerals are mined underground by the room-and-pillar method. About a dozen countries produce potassium minerals, the leaders being Canada, East Germany, West Germany, the United States, and France. The U.S. production comes from mines about 20 miles (32 kilometers) east of Carlsbad, New Mexico. The product that goes to the market is purified potassium chloride, KCl. See also **POTASH.** (2, 5)

PROSPECTING. Searching for economically valuable deposits of minerals or mineral fuels. See also **EXPLORATION** and **PROSPECTOR.**

PROSPECTOR. A person looking for valuable mineral deposits, generally working alone and with simple tools or portable detectors. The term implies an individual searching on his own behalf, not a mining-company employee.

PUMICE. A light-colored, glassy igneous rock that is full of gas-bubble holes. Though extremely porous, pumice is not permeable because the voids are sealed off from one another; most pumice will float on water. The rock is formed when masses of silica-rich lava are thrown violently from a volcanic vent and cool rapidly. Crushed and screened pumice is useful as a lightweight aggregate and as an abrasive.

PYRITE. A common yellow metallic mineral, chemical name iron sulfide (FeS_2). Pyrite is a minor ore of iron but is more important as an ore of sulfur, especially in Europe. Synonym: **FOOL'S GOLD.**

Q

QUARRY. A surface excavation from which rock is extracted. Dimension stone, crushed stone, and cement raw materials are commonly quarried.

QUARTZ. A mineral composed entirely of silica, which is the chemical compound silicon dioxide (SiO_2). Quartz is the second most common mineral in the earth's crust, after feldspar. It occurs in hard gray or white grains and crystalline masses in many igneous and metamorphic rocks. It is also the commonest gangue mineral of ore deposits. Quartz grains are the dominant material of sand, sandstone, and quartzite.

Very thin plates of clear, flawless crystalline quartz in radio and other communication systems ensure narrow frequency channels, keeping signals on the beam. In watches, the energy from a battery makes a tiny plate of quartz vibrate at a very fast and steady rate, and the vibrations are translated into time. Most of the quartz used is synthetically grown, using small amounts of clear natural quartz as the starting material or seed.

QUARTZITE. A sedimentary or metamorphic rock made of quartz grains cemented together by quartz. High-purity quartzite is a raw material of elemental silicon, glass, and ferrosilicon. It is produced in Ontario and California.

QUICKLIME. Lime: calcium oxide, CaO.

QUICKSILVER. Mercury, Hg.

R

RADIOACTIVE WASTES. Material from atomic reactors that is radioactive and for which there is no further use. Spent nuclear fuel, classed as a high-level waste, is harmful and will remain so for hundreds of years. Sealed in glass or otherwise stabilized, these wastes will eventually have to be buried. There are serious technical problems connected with burial, such as preventing the wastes from polluting underground water supplies and locating the burial site far from earthquake zones, where disruption might occur. Even more difficult are social and political problems. No community wants radioactive wastes buried nearby. Some states even object to allowing transport of such wastes on their highways. To select a burial site that pleases everyone has proved impossible. In the late 1980s, geologic studies were being undertaken at Yucca Mountain, Nevada, as a possible site; but even if this remote area is shown to be physically suitable, it is by no means certain that citizens concerned with the environment will permit its approval.

About 35 tons of high-level wastes per nuclear power plant accumulate each year. Low-level wastes, such as air filters and laboratory equipment, do not present serious disposal problems.

RADIUM (Ra). A metallic element that occurs in very small amounts in uranium-bearing minerals. On disintegration, radium produces radon and helium.

RADON. A rare radioactive gas produced by the disintegration of radium. It is a health hazard (as a cause of lung cancer) for workers at uranium mines and mills. Radon is present in ordinary rocks and soils, but in such small amounts that it is believed to present little or no health risk.

RARE EARTHS. A series of fifteen metallic elements, ranging from lanthanum, La (atomic number 57) to lutetium, Lu (71), together with three other elements: yttrium, Y; thorium, Th; and scandium, Sc. These elements are not especially rare in the earth's crust, but concentrations of them are. Economic amounts are present in two phosphate minerals, monazite and xenotime, and in one carbonate mineral, bastnaesite. Monazite and xenotime are heavy minerals and occur with titanium minerals in the beach sands of Western Australia. Bastnaesite is mined at Mountain Pass, California. Australia and the United States produce more than 90 percent of the world's output of rare earths. Various compounds of the group are used as catalysts in oil refining; also in high-strength magnets, ceramics and glass, special alloys, phosphors for color TV, and in a number of other products. Ceramic superconducting materials, composed of the oxides of certain metals and rare earths, will operate at much higher temperatures than conventional superconducting materials.

An environmental concern in mining monazite-bearing placers along beaches is the possible conflict with urban and recreational land use and damage to undeveloped areas. Although mine reclamation has been successful in Australia, public concern has limited the availability of minable deposits.

RECLAMATION. The restoration of land that has been disturbed by mining or quarrying. Most states now require operators to restore the surface for recreational or other use. In stripping for coal, the topsoil may be stockpiled separately from the rest of the overburden; it is then redistributed on the restored surface and planted as desired. Operators of big stripping machines in the Florida phosphate field have detailed instructions on replacing overburden so as to leave an area that can readily be landscaped. Worked-out gravel pits are the sites of ponds, schools, or playgrounds; a few large ones are now landfills. Former quarries have been converted to use as public gardens.

RECYCLING. Recovery and reuse. In the mineral industries it is largely confined to certain metals. The recycling of scrap iron and steel, for example, is a major subdivision of the steel industry. In addition, in 1987 about 850,000 tons of aluminum cans, 520,000 tons of copper wire and sheet, and 630,000 tons of lead from scrap batteries were recycled. The mineral fuels and most of the nonmetallics are used up the first time around, and so produce no scrap. However, one product of the mineral industry, namely glass, is routinely recycled as part of the charge of raw materials to the glassmaking furnace.

Recycling allows the metal producer to start with already refined metal rather than crude ore, thus saving much energy. It also decreases the amount of waste that must be handled by communities and industries. Recycling is thus a double money-saver.

RESERVES. That part of the total resources of a rock, mineral, or fossil fuel that can be produced profitably under present economic conditions. Reserves are identified and measured by drilling and mapping ahead of production. The remaining life of a mine or oil pool can be calculated by dividing reserves by rate of production. See also **RESOURCES.**

RESERVOIR ROCK. A subsurface body of porous and permeable rock that contains oil, gas, or both, in a pool. The reservoir rock is overlain by the roof rock of the pool. Informal synonyms: oil sand; gas sand. See also **OIL POOL** and **TRAP**.

RESOURCES. The reserves of a mineral or of a fossil fuel, plus known deposits that are not economically recoverable now but may be in the future, plus deposits that are inferred to exist but have not yet been discovered. The concept of resources is used at the regional or national level, as for example in calculating the copper resources of the western United States or the coal resources of Antarctica. See also **RESERVES.**

RHENIUM (Re). A rare metallic element that is produced as a byproduct of copper and molybdenum refining. Its major use is in platinum-rhenium catalysts that increase the octane rating of lead-free gasoline. Other uses are in heating elements, X-ray tubes, and flash-bulbs.

ROCK SALT. Salt.

ROCK WOOL. Mineral wool.

ROOF ROCK. The impermeable rock lying on the reservoir rock of an oil or gas pool. It acts as a barrier to upward migration of the oil or gas. One of the most common and effective roof rocks is shale. See also **OIL POOL** and **TRAP.**

ROOM-AND-PILLAR MINING. A method of underground mining, generally in flat-lying rocks, in which the rock is removed in rooms separated by pillars of undisturbed rock left for roof support. Some room-and-pillar mines have been converted, once mining was completed, into underground storage areas, machine shops, and even offices.

ROTARY DRILLING. A method of drilling wells in which a drill pipe with a bit at the bottom is rotated from the surface. Ground-up rock is removed from the bottom of the hole by a circulating fluid. See also **DRILLING FLUID.**

RUBIDIUM (Rb). A metallic element that is extremely reactive. It is produced in very small quantities from a pegmatite ore imported from Canada. Rubidium compounds are used mainly in research and development. See also **CESIUM.**

S

SALT. A white or gray crystalline rock made almost entirely of the mineral halite. Salt is a major industrial raw material, for both of its constituent elements, sodium and chlorine, have scores of applications. Salt is also used for de-icing roads, in water softening, and for preserving and flavoring food. Beds of salt, formed by evaporation of ancient seas, are mined in the New York / Ohio / Michigan / Ontario region, in central Kansas, and elsewhere in North America, as well as in Western Europe. Salt is also obtained by evaporating sea water, which contains 3.5 percent NaCl. See also **HALITE** and **SALT DOME.** (12)

SALT DOME. A column of salt that has pushed its way upward for thousands of feet from a salt bed through overlying sediments. Salt domes are so called because they tend to arch the rock layers above them, not because they are domelike themselves.

On the Gulf Coast of the United States, a thick bed of salt has been buried by as much as 40,000 feet (12,000 meters) of sand and clay. These sediments accumulated as the region slowly sank and the Mississippi and other rivers poured sand and mud from the continental interior into the sea. The mother salt bed is too deep to be reached by drilling, but is known to exist from regional and geophysical studies, as well as from the evidence of the salt domes. Two factors make this sediment-on-salt situation unstable. First, the layers of sand and clay are heavier than the salt below them. Second, salt is a weak crystalline solid, which flows readily when stressed in the earth's crust. It flows in solid form, like the ice in a glacier. Apparently, bulges or points of weakness on the upper surface of the salt layer finally gave way, and at these places salt began to move upward, slowly but steadily, through the layers of sediment. The most common form taken by the salt is a column or plug, roughly circular in cross section, averaging less than a mile in diameter, and reaching a point between a few feet and a few hundred feet from the surface. More than two hundred fifty salt domes are known in the Louisiana-Texas portion of the Gulf Coast. Lying directly on the salt of most domes is a layer of anhydrite and impure limestone, termed the caprock.

Salt domes are threefold mineral resources. First, oil and gas occur in porous sandstone beds tilted upward around the salt plug; in cavernous limestone of the caprock; and in domed overlying strata. The number and variety of oil and gas traps associated with salt domes has made the Gulf Coast one of the most productive petroleum provinces in North America. Second, the salt itself is mined at several domes. Large caverns may be excavated. At a few domes where salt mining has ceased, the cavities are now used for underground storage of crude oil. Third, at a few domes deposits of native sulfur are found in the impure limestone of the caprock. The sulfur is recovered by the Frasch method.

The salt-dome province of the Gulf Coast extends seaward, as evidenced by extensive offshore drilling for oil and gas in the Gulf of Mexico. Clusters of salt domes are known in several other regions, notably in the North German Coastal Plan. See also **FRASCH METHOD.**

SAND. A loose granular sediment whose particles range from 0.0025 to 0.008 inch (0.625–2 mm) in diameter. Quartz is the dominant material of most sand, and essentially the only one in the high-silica sand used in glassmaking. Quartz sand is used as concrete aggregate, in filtering water supplies, in sandblasting, and as fracturing sand. Some sands contain valuable amounts of heavy minerals.

SANDSTONE. A sedimentary rock made of sand grains, dominantly quartz, cemented by calcite, iron oxide, or clay. High-purity sandstone that is weakly cemented and can readily be broken down into sand is the basic raw material of glass. Porous and permeable sandstone is the reservoir rock of many oil pools.

SCANDIUM (Sc). A metallic element occurring with elements of the rare-earth group. It is obtained as a minor byproduct in the processing of the ores of fluorite, copper and molybdenum. The principal uses for scandium are in laser rods and high-intensity mercury-vapor lamps.

SEAM. A particular bed or vein in a series. The term usually refers to coal, but it may be used for other mineral deposits.

SECONDARY RECOVERY. A general term for several techniques that have been developed for increasing the total amount of oil recovered from a pool. For example, water may be pumped into the reservoir rock through specially drilled wells so that it will push oil ahead of it toward the producing wells.

SEISMIC PROSPECTING. A technique that gives geologists information about subsurface rocks in exploring for oil and gas. A series of geophones, connected to a recording device, is spaced out along a line on the ground. An explosion is then set off to produce a mini-earthquake. The shock waves travel downward into the crust. Each resistant rock layer reflects some of the wave energy back to the surface, and the geophones pick up these reflected waves. The resulting seismogram shows the attitude and thickness of the rocks down to a depth of several thousand feet.

SELENIUM. (Se). A gray nonmetallic element of the sulfur group. It is used in electronic devices and photocopiers, because its electrical conductivity varies with the intensity of light. Selenium is a coloring agent of red glass. It is a byproduct in the refining of copper.

SHAFT. A passage, vertical or inclined, extending from the surface to a body of rock being mined.

SHALE. A sedimentary rock made of consolidated clay or mud. Certain shales are suitable for use in making brick and tile. When crushed and heated, a few shales will expand or bloat to product lightweight aggregate for concrete.

SILICA. Known also as the compound silicon dioxide (SiO_2). Its most common form is the mineral quartz, but silica also makes up chert, flint, opal, diatomite, and several other earth materials. Silicon and oxygen, the components of silica, are the two most abundant elements in the earth's crust. Adjective: **SILICEOUS.**

SILICON (Si). A nonmetallic element that is the second most abundant element in the earth's crust (after oxygen). Silicon occurs only in combination with oxygen, as in quartz and its relatives (SiO_2) and in many silicate minerals (in the combining form SiO_4). Silicon, produced from pure quartzite or quartz sand, is combined with iron to form ferrosilicon, used in steelmaking; and with carbon to form silicon carbide, a hard abrasive. High-purity silicon is used in memory chips for computers.

SILVER. (**Ag**, from the Latin *argentum*). A soft white metal. Silver is used in photography, electrical products, sterling tableware, jewelry, and coins. A major United States producer is a deep mine near Kellogg, Idaho, where silver-bearing sulfide minerals occur in quartz veins. Silver is also produced as a byproduct at about forty gold mines.

SLAG. Molten material drawn off from the blast furnace in the smelting of iron ore. It consists of phosphorus, silica, and other impurities, combined with the flux that was introduced with the ore. Once considered a waste material, cooled and hardened slag is now crushed, screened, and used in concrete aggregate.

SLATE. A metamorphic rock that has resulted from the intense folding and mild metamorphism of shale. Most slate is black or gray, but some is red or various shades of green. Slate has well-developed rock cleavage, and can be split into the slabs and thin plates commonly used for roofing and flooring.

SLIME. A term used in the Florida phosphate district for a mixture of water and clay, a waste produce of phosphate-rock concentration. Slime will not separate into its constituent parts, even over long periods, so it must be stored indefinitely in slime ponds behind earthen dams. The ponds take up land and must be monitored to be sure the dams do not break. Much research has been devoted, so far without success, to devising a cheap way of causing the clay and water to separate.

SLURRY. A free-flowing mixture of water and finely ground material such as clay, coal, or cement.

SMELTING. Melting or fusing ore to separate the metal from associated impurities. The process is generally aided by the use of a flux. See also **SLAG.**

SODA ASH. The commercial name for the chemical compound sodium carbonate (Na_2CO_3). Soda ash is a prime ingredient of glass, and about half of the soda ash produced is used in glassmaking.

About a quarter goes into various chemicals, and the remainder is used in soaps and detergents, water treatment, and paper manufacture. Soda ash in the United States, formerly manufactured, is now derived from naturally occurring deposits. See **SOLVAY PROCESS** and **TRONA.**

SODIUM SULFATE (Na_2SO_4). This compound has three main uses: in detergents, pulp and paper, and glass. More than half of the sodium sulfate is synthetic, being a byproduct of various chemical and rayon manufacturing facilities. The remainder is derived from brines that saturate the salt beds of dry lakes, or from two minerals of such lakes: thenardite, Na_2SO_4, and its high-hydrate relative, mirabilite, $Na_2SO_4 \cdot 10H_2O$. Many countries are producers of sodium sulfate.

SOLUTION MINING. A technique of obtaining salt by drilling wells into a buried salt bed, forcing water down to dissolve the salt, and pumping the resulting brine to the surface. The brine may be evaporated to yield solid salt, or introduced into processes of chemical manufacture. At one locality, potassium minerals are produced by solution mining.

SOLVAY PROCESS. A process for manufacturing sodium carbonate (soda ash). A salt brine is saturated with ammonia, carbon dioxide is passed through it, and a sodium-bicarbonate slurry is formed. The bicarbonate is filtered from the liquid and calcined to form sodium carbonate, Na_2CO_3. The process is named for Ernest Solvay, a Belgian chemist.

SOURCE ROCK. The rock in which oil and gas originated. There is no general agreement on what this rock is, except that it was once a sediment rich in the remains of primitive marine organisms.

STOCKPILE. A reserve supply of metals or minerals kept by a government to guard against future shortages or emergency. See also **STRATEGIC MINERALS.**

STONE. 1. Informal term for an individual diamond, ruby, or other gem; a precious stone. 2. Rock put to physical use. See also **CRUSHED STONE** and **DIMENSION STONE.**

STOPE. An underground excavation formed by the extraction of ore.

STOPING. Extraction of ore in a mine by working laterally along a vein in a series of levels or steps. It is generally done from lower to upper levels. The term stoping is sometimes used in a general sense to mean the extraction of ore.

STRATEGIC MINERALS. Minerals that are considered vital to the security of a nation, but that must be procured mostly or entirely from foreign sources because domestic production will not meet requirements in time of war. Chromium- and tin-bearing minerals and sheet mica, among others, were designated strategic minerals during World War II. See also **STOCKPILE.**

STRIP MINING. Extraction of phosphate rock, sand and gravel, and especially coal, from flat extensive deposits at or near the surface. At a typical strip mine for coal, the rock overlying the coal bed is first loosened by mild blasting. It is then scooped up by immense machines, called draglines, that deposit the material in a worked-out area. The coal is then removed by power shovels. In some Appalachian coal fields, more than one hundred feet (30.5 meters) of overburden is removed in order to get at a bed of coal 4 feet (1.2 meters) thick.

Until the 1960s, strip mining was done with little or no regard for damage to the land surface, and in some regions it is still done in this way. Generally, however, companies are required to restore the land to productive use as mining is completed. See also **RECLAMATION.**

STRONTIUM (Sr). A metallic element found only in combination with other elements. Its chief ore mineral is celestite (strontium sulfate, $SrSO_4$). Celestite is the starting point for the manufacture of strontium carbonate and other compounds. More than half of the strontium is consumed in making the glass face plates of color television tubes, and much of the remainder in firewords and signals. The United States produces no strontium minerals. Celestite is imported from Mexico, and strontium compounds from West Germany, Mexico, and Spain.

SULFUR (S). A bright yellow nonmetallic element that occurs in native form. It is also found in combination with many metallic elements, as sulfides such as pyrite, FeS_2, and as sulfates such as anhydrite, $CaSO_4$. Although we seldom or never encounter sulfur in everyday life, this element is used at some stage in the production of practically everything we eat, wear, or use. Sulfur enters manufacturing processes most commonly in the form of sulfuric acid, H_2SO_4. This compound has so many industrial uses that it is known as the king of chemicals. Sulfur or its acid is used in making paper, rayon, film, auto tires, paint, detergents, explosives, matches, food, drugs, and dyes. Sulfuric acid is also essential in the manufacture of phosphate fertilizer for the world's croplands.

Native sulfur, also known as brimstone, occurs in granular masses in the caprock of certain salt domes, and in a few bedded deposits. From both of these types of accumulation it is recovered in liquid form via wells. Frasch sulfur dominated the industry from around the beginning of the century to the 1960s. Since then, however, an increasing proportion of sulfur has come from two other sources. The first is hydrogen sulfide, H_2S, a gas that occurs with crude oil and natural gas in many pools and must be separated from them before they can be put in the pipeline to refinery or market. Recovering elemental sulfur from H_2S has involved a number of oil companies with the sulfur business. The second current source is sulfur dioxide, SO_2, recovered from the stack gases of smelters, manufacturing plants, and especially coal-burning power plants. Production of sulfur from H_2S and SO_2 now far outranks production from the native element.

Other sources of sulfur have been important in the past. One of these was bright yellow native sulfur that accumulates around volcanic vents on the island of Sicily. Another source has been deposits of the mineral pyrite, which can be roasted to separate sulfur from its companion element, iron.

From time to time a surplus of sulfur has developed, and research has been undertaken to find additional uses. The most interesting of these possibilities is in sulfur concrete. A paste consisting of mineral fillers, melted sulfur, and air replaces the water-cement paste of ordinary concrete. After addition of aggregate, the sulfur concrete is heated to 130°–160° C (266°–320° F). When the mixture is cooled, the sulfur binds it into a strong and durable material that is highly resistant to weather, acid, and salt. See also **FRASCH METHOD.** (16)

T

TACONITE. A dark red siliceous iron ore present in the iron-mining districts of northern Minnesota and Michigan. Taconite is a low-grade ore, containing 25 to 30 percent of hematite (Fe_2O_3) and magnetite (Fe_3O_4). Fine grinding and magnetic treatment produce a concentrate containing 62 to 65 percent iron, a grade suitable for the blast furnace. See also **PELLETIZING.**

TALC. A soft, slippery light-colored mineral, a magnesium silicate. Talc is so soft that it can be scratched with the fingernail. It grinds to a brilliant white powder. In paint, its softness helps with smooth flow and its opacity adds hiding power to cover older surfaces. Powdered talc is also used in porcelain and other high-grade ceramics and as a filler in plastics and paper; the very highest grades appear on the cosmetics shelf as talcum powder. Talc is a mineral of metamorphic rocks. It is mined in California, Montana, New York, Vermont, and Texas, and in more than a dozen countries outside the United States.

TAILINGS. The part of milled ore that is left as waste after extraction of the desired mineral. Finely ground tailings in water suspension are commonly piped to artificial ponds, where they settle out and leave reusable water.

TANTALUM (Ta). A rare corrosion-resistant metallic element. It has a variety of uses in electronic components, carbides, corrosion-resistant alloys, and other equipment. Most of the world's production of tantalum takes place outside the United States; Brazil, Australia, and Thailand are major producers. The chief ore mineral is tantalite, $(Fe,Mn)(Ta,Nb)_2O_6$. It occurs typically in pegmatites.

TAR. Coal tar.

TELLURIUM (Te). A rare tin-white nonmetallic element of the sulfur group. It is alloyed with iron, copper, and lead, and is a component of semiconductors. Tellurium is obtained as a byproduct in the refining of copper.

THALLIUM (Ti). A rare metallic element obtained from the flue dusts and residues in the smelting of copper, zinc, and lead ores. Thallium is light-sensitive and is used in photoelectric cells; also in pharmaceuticals, alloys, and glassmaking. It is extremely toxic when breathed or ingested; at one time it was used in rat and insect poisons.

THORIUM (Th). A rare radioactive element that is generally grouped with the rare earths. It is used as nuclear fuel (though in much smaller amounts than uranium), and various compounds of thorium go into incandescent lamps, magnesium-thorium alloys, refractories, ceramics, and other products. Thorium is obtained from the mineral monazite, a rare-earth phosphate with thorium substituting for rare earths. Some monazite is mined on a small scale from sands in Florida, but most is imported from Australia. See also **RARE EARTHS.**

TIN (Sn, from the Latin *stannum*). A silver-white metallic element. It is an important metal in alloys. With lead, it forms easily melted solder, used to join or patch metal parts or surfaces; with copper, it forms bronze. The tin can is made of sheet steel with a thin coating of tin. The chief tin mineral of commerce is the oxide cassiterite, SnO_2, which is found as a heavy mineral in placer deposits. The United States imports most of its tin. Important producers include Brazil, Thailand, Indonesia, and Bolivia. The world supply of tin is greater than the demand.

TITANIUM MINERALS. Two dark, heavy oxides of the metallic element titanium (symbol: Ti). These are ilmenite, $FeTiO_3$, and rutile, TiO_2. Titanium metal derived from these minerals is used in jet engines, airframes, and missiles. However, about 90 percent of titanium-mineral production is used in the manufacture of titanium dioxide, TiO_2. Unlike its natural form, rutile, refined and purified TiO_2 is brilliant white. In powdered form it is used in paper and plastics, but by far its most important use is in paint pigment. The titanium minerals are obtained mainly from beach sands along the western coast of Australia. They are heavy minerals and are readily separated from the dominant quartz sand by gravity methods.

TRAP. Any underground condition that causes oil and gas to accumulate in a pool. Oil and gas normally move upward through rocks because they are lighter than the water that saturates rocks in the subsurface. A trap is any barrier to this upward migration, and consists of a roof rock overlying the porous reservoir rock that holds the oil or gas. A trap may be formed by a gentle arching of the rocks, by a fault, by a change in rock permeability, or in a variety of other ways. See also **OIL POOL, RESERVOIR ROCK,** and **ROOF ROCK.**

TRAPROCK. Commercial name for crushed basalt, used as aggregate in concrete.

TRONA. A clear to white crystalline mineral that consists of hydrous sodium carbonate ($Na_2CO_3 \cdot NaHCO_3 \cdot 2H_2O$). Trona is mined by several companies from underground beds in southwestern Wyoming. The mineral was formed in a shallow lake, probably by evaporation. Trona is the source of sodium carbonate in the United States. See also **SODA ASH** and **SOLVAY PROCESS.**

TUBING. The pipe, generally 4 to 6 inches (10 to 15 centimeters) in diameter, through which oil, gas, or both flow from an underground pool to the surface. Tubing is placed inside the casing.

TUNGSTEN (**W**, from the German *Wolfram*). A hard gray metallic element. It is alloyed with carbon to produce tungsten carbide, a very hard substance used in drill bits and high-speed cutting tools. Tungsten is also used in filaments for light bulbs. The chief ore mineral is wolframite, an iron-manganese tungstate, $(Fe,Mn)WO_4$. Wolframite occurs as crystalline and granular masses in veins. United States production is minor; imports come from Canada, China, Bolivia, and several other countries.

U

UNDERCLAY. Soft clayey material immediately beneath many beds of bituminous coal. It is thought to be the soil, much altered, in which the coal-making plants grew. Underclays range from a few inches to a few feet thick. Thicker beds yield clay for making brick and tile.

URANIUM (U). A heavy radioactive metallic element. It is used almost entirely in nuclear technology. One of uranium's three isotopes (forms with different atomic weights) is U-235. Although U-235 makes up only 0.7 percent of naturally occurring uranium, it is of great value because it undergoes fission. In this process, an atomic nucleus splits into two smaller nuclei of about the same size, releasing energy. A controlled nuclear reaction yields heat to generate steam and drive turbines for electric power. An uncontrolled reaction produces the explosion of an atomic bomb. The chief ore mineral of uranium is the oxide uraninite, UO_2, or a variety known as pitchblende, U_3O_8. These ideal compositions are almost always modified by a content of thorium, vanadium, or rare earths. Uraninite is a dark gray metallic mineral that occurs in veins and sulfide deposits in the Congo Basin of Africa, at Great Bear Lake in northwestern Canada, and in a few other places. Uranium has also been obtained from a yellow oxide mineral, carnotite, which occurs in certain sandstones in Colorado, Utah, and New Mexico.

Uranium is chemically toxic, and radiation can cause cancer and genetic defects. A hazard at mines and mills is the radioactive gas radon. See also **RADIOACTIVE WASTES.** (6)

V

VANADIUM (V). A silver-white metallic element. It is used chiefly as an alloy in high-strength steel. No mineral deposits are worked solely for vanadium. It is a minor constituent of some uranium ores, from which it is recovered as a byproduct. Vanadium is also obtained from phosphate rock, petroleum residue, power plant ash, and slag.

VEIN. The mineral matter that fills a fault or other fracture, differing in composition from the surrounding host rock. Veins are generally sheetlike in form. They may or may not contain valuable ore minerals. Most vein material is deposited from hydrothermal solutions. See also **LODE.**

VERMICULITE. A brown or black flaky silicate material, formed in nature by the weathering of biotite (black mica). Vermiculite contains a little combined water. When grains are exposed for a few seconds to temperatures of 800°–1200° C (1472°–2192° F), their water flashes into steam, and the grains expand to from fifteen to thirty times in volume. Expansion takes place at right angles to the plane of cleavage; it resembles the opening-out of an accordion. Some of the resulting particles are curved. The resemblance of these particles to worms gives vermiculite its name (Latin, little-worm stone). Expanded vermiculite is used as loose-fill insulation, in lightweight concrete and plaster, and as a rooting agent and soil conditioner. Much of the United States' supply comes from a deposit in northwestern Montana; there are other deposits in South Carolina and Virginia. The mineral is shipped in crude form and expanded near the places where it is to be used.

VOLATILE MATTER. In coal, those substances other than moisture that are given off as gas and vapor when the coal burns. Standardized laboratory methods are used in determining volatile matter, along with moisture, ash, and fixed carbon.

VOLCANIC ASH. Finely pulverized rock from an explosive volcanic eruption. Despite its name, it is not a product of burning. Certain beds of volcanic ash have been altered by weathering to form bentonite; others are the host rock of the beryllium mineral, bertrandite.

W

WELL LOG. A graphic record of the rocks encountered in a well. It is plotted on a strip of paper to scale (for example, 1 inch on the log strip = 100 feet in the well). Well logs may be based on a geologist's description of the rock cuttings or cores from the well, or they may show the electrical resistivity, radioactivity, or other properties of the rocks as determined by instruments. Well logs are valuable tools in exploring for minerals, water, and especially oil and gas.

WHITE SMOKER. A vent in the sea floor from which a plume or jet of white hydrothermal fluid pours into the ocean water. The fluid is clouded by white precipitates, mostly silica and barite. It issues at a rate of tens of centimeters per second and at temperatures of 100° C to 350° C (212° F to 662° F). Some barite deposits may have originated in white smokers. See also **BLACK SMOKER.**

WILDCAT WELL. A well drilled at a distance from known deposits of oil or gas, in the hope of discovering a new pool. It is so-called because in the early days of the oil industry drillers on wells back in the hills said they were working out among the wildcats.

WOLLASTONITE. A white to yellowish-brown mineral, chemical name calcium silicate ($CaSiO_3$). Finely ground, it is used in such ceramics as wall tile and electric insulators, and as a filler in rubber and plastics. Wollastonite is a metamorphic mineral, commonly occurring with garnet. A major United States deposit is in the eastern Adirondack Mountains of New York.

Y

YTTRIUM (Y). A metallic element occurring with the rare-earth group of elements. It is obtained from the carbonate mineral bastnaesite, mined in California, and from the phosphate mineral monazite, obtained from beach sands in Western Australia. Yttrium metal and its compounds are used in phosphors for color TV and computer monitoring screens; in laser crystals and glass; and in superalloys and advanced ceramic materials.

Z

ZEOLITES. A group of minerals that are hydrous silicates of aluminum with calcium, sodium, or potassium. Their value rests on their molecular structure or framework. When the combined water of a zeolite is removed by heating, as much as 50 percent of the framework consists of open spaces. As these spaces have rigid dimensions, they will allow molecules of certain substances to be taken in, or absorbed, but will exclude larger molecules. Thus the zeolite acts as a molecular sieve. This property is used in numerous processes, including oil refining. Zeolites are mined on a small scale from beds of volcanic ash east of Tucson, Arizona. The market for natural zeolites is limited because synthetic zeolites are firmly established in industry.

ZINC (Zn). A bluish white metallic element. It is used in plating, or galvanizing, iron and other metals for protection against corrosion; in alloys, such as brass; and in chemicals and medicines. Zinc's chief ore mineral is the sulfide sphalerite (ZnS). Sphalerite typically occurs in veins and replacement bodies in limestone, often accompanied by galena (PbS), the ore mineral of lead. Zinc is also a byproduct of gold and silver production. Most United States zinc comes from mines in Missouri, Tennessee, and New York.

ZIRCON. A yellow or brown mineral, chemical name zirconium silicate ($ZrSiO_4$). Two-thirds of the output is used as foundry sands and refractories, and most of the rest in ceramics and abrasives. In 1987 a golf putter was developed with a head fashioned of zirconia (ZrO_2) ceramic. Zircon is the source of the elements zirconium and hafnium, which have uses in nuclear reactors and metal alloys. Transparent varieties of zircon make brilliant gemstones. Zircon occurs in Australian beach sands, and is produced as a coproduct with the titanium minerals ilmenite and rutile.

ZONING. 1. In urban planning, restriction of certain areas for specialized development, such as residential, industrial, or recreational. 2. In ore deposits, the distribution patterns of elements or minerals. For example, a vein may be made up of several zones, each with a characteristic mineral composition.

FOR FURTHER INFORMATION

NATIONAL AGENCIES

Minerals Information Office
Mail Stop 2647-MIB
U.S. Department of the Interior
18th and C Streets NW
Washington, DC 20240

Visitor Center:
2600 Corridor
E Street Entrance
Interior Building
18th and E Streets NW
Washington, DC

Occupational Health and Safety Administration
200 Constitution Avenue NW
Washington, DC 20210

Geological Survey of Canada
601 Booth Street, Room 665
Ottawa, Ontario K1A OE8
Canada

INSTITUTES

American Geological Institute
4220 King Street
Alexandria, VA 22302–1507

Minerals Information Institute
6565 South Dayton Street
Suite 3800
Englewood, CO 80111

INDUSTRY GROUPS

American Coal Foundation
918 16th Street NW
Washington, DC 20006–2902

American Mining Congress
1920 N Street NW
Washington, DC 20036

American Petroleum Institute
1220 L Street NW
Washington, DC 20005

National Aggregates Association
900 Spring Street
Silver Spring, MD 20910

National Stone Association
1415 Elliott Place NW
Washington, DC 20007

STATE GEOLOGICAL SURVEYS

Geological Survey of Alabama
Box 0, University Station
Tuscaloosa, AL 35486

**Alaska Division of Geological
and Geophysical Surveys**
3700 Airport Way
Fairbanks, AK 99709

Arizona Geological Survey
845 North Park Ave.
Tucson, AZ 85719

Arkansas Geological Commission
3815 West Roosevelt Rd.
Little Rock, AR 72204

**California Division of Mines and
Geology**
1416 Ninth St., Room 1341
Sacramento, CA 95814

Colorado Geological Survey
1313 Sherman St., Room 715
Denver, CO 80203

**Connecticut Geological &
Natural History Survey**
State Office Bldg., Room 553
Hartford, CT 06106

Delaware Geological Survey
DGS Building
University of Delaware
Newark, DE 19716

Florida Geological Survey
903 West Tennessee St.
Tallahassee, FL 32304

Georgia Geologic Survey
19 Martin Luther King Dr. SW
Atlanta, GA 30334

**Hawaii Division of Water &
Resource Management**
Box 373
Honolulu, HI 96809

Idaho Geological Survey
University of Idaho
332 Morrill Hall
Moscow, ID 83843

Illinois Geological Survey
615 East Peabody Drive
Champaign, IL 61820

Indiana Geological Survey
611 North Walnut Grove
Bloomington, IN 47405

Iowa Geological Survey
123 North Capitol St.
Iowa City, IA 52242

Kansas Geological Survey
1930 Constant Ave.
West Campus
University of Kansas
Lawrence, KS 66047

Kentucky Geological Survey
228 Mining and Mineral
Resources Building
University of Kentucky
Lexington, KY 40506

Louisiana Geological Survey
Box G, University Station
Baton Rouge, LA 70893

Maine Geological Survey
State House Station 22
Augusta, ME 04333

Maryland Geological Survey
2300 St. Paul St.
Baltimore, MD 21218

Massachusetts Office of
Environmental Affairs
100 Cambridge St.
Boston, MA 02202

Michigan Geological Survey
Box 30028
Lansing, MI 48909

Minnesota Geological Survey
2642 University Ave.
St. Paul, MN 55114–1507

Mississippi Bureau of Geology
Box 5348
Jackson, MS 39296

Missouri Division of Geology
and Land Survey
Box 250
Rolla, MO 65401

Montana Bureau of Mines &
Geology
Montana College of Mineral
Science and Technology
Butte, MT 59701

Nebraska Conservation &
Survey Division
113 Nebraska Hall
University of Nebraska
Lincoln, NE 68588–0517

Nevada Bureau of Mines
& Geology
University of Nevada
Reno, NV 89557–0088

New Hampshire Geological
Survey
117 James Hall
University of New Hampshire
Durham, NH 03824

New Jersey Geological Survey
P.O. Box CN-029
Trenton, NJ 08625

New Mexico Bureau of Mines &
Mineral Resources
Campus Station
Socorro, NM 87801

New York State
Geological Survey
3136 Cultural Education Center
Empire State Plaza
Albany, NY 12230

North Carolina Geological
Survey
Box 27687
Raleigh, NC 27611

North Dakota Geological Survey
600 East Blvd.
Grand Forks, ND 58505

Ohio Division of
Geological Survey
4383 Fountain Square Drive
Columbus, OH 43224

Oklahoma Geological Survey
100 East Boyd
Norman, OK 73019

Oregon Department of Geology
& Mineral Industries
910 State Office Building
1400 SW 5th Ave.
Portland, OR 97201–5528

Pennsylvania Bureau of
Topographic & Geologic Survey
Box 2357
Harrisburg, PA 17120

Puerto Rico Department of
Natural Resources
Box 5887
Puerta de Tierra Station
San Juan, PR 00906

Rhode Island Statewide
Planning Program
Dept. of Geology
University of Rhode Island
Kingston, RI 02881

South Carolina
Geological Survey
5 Geology Road
Columbia, SC 29210

South Dakota Geological Survey
University of South Dakota
Vermillion, SD 57069–2390

Tennessee Division of Geology
701 Broadway
Nashville, TN 37243

Texas Bureau of
Economic Geology
Box X, University Station
Austin, TX 78712–7508

Utah Geological &
Mineral Survey
606 Black Hawk Way
Salt Lake City, UT 84108–1280

Vermont Geological Survey
103 South Main St.
Waterbury, VT 05676

Virginia Division of
Mineral Resources
Box 3667
Charlottesville, VA 22903

Washington Division of
Geology & Earth Resources
Dept. of Natural Resources
Olympia, WA 98504

West Virginia Geological &
Economic Survey
Mont Chateau Research Center
Box 879
Morgantown, WV 26507–0879

Wisconsin Geological &
Natural History Survey
3817 Mineral Point Rd.
Madison, WI 53705

Wyoming Geological Survey
Box 3008, University Station
Laramie, WY 82071

CANADIAN PROVINCIAL SURVEYS

Alberta Geological Survey
Box 8330 Postal Station F
Edmonton, Alberta T6H 5X2

Geological Survey Branch
200–756 Fort Street
Victoria, British Columbia
V8W 3A3

Geological Services Branch,
Manitoba Energy & Mines
555–330 Graham Ave.
Winnipeg, Manitoba R3C 4E3

New Brunswick Minerals &
Energy Division
Box 6000
Fredericton, New Brunswick
E3B 5H1

Newfoundland Department of
Mines & Energy
Box 8700
St. John's, Newfoundland A1B 4J6

Geology Division, Northern
Affairs Program
Box 1500
Yellowknife, Northwest
Territories X1A 2R3

Nova Scotia Department of
Mines & Energy
Box 1087
Halifax, Nova Scotia B3J 2X1

Ontario Geological Survey,
Ministry of Natural Resources
77 Grenville St.
Toronto, Ontario M7A 1W4

Department of Energy &
Minerals
Box 2000
Charlottetown, Prince Edward
Island C1A 7N8

Ministry of Energy & Resources
5700 4th Avenue West
Charlesbourg, Quebec G1H 6R1

Saskatchewan Energy & Mines
1914 Hamilton St.
Regina, Saskatchewan S4P 4V4

Exploration & Geological
Services Division
200 Range Road, Whitehorse
Yukon Territory Y1A 3V1

REFERENCES

BOOKS

1. Bates, R. L., *The Challenge of Mineral Resources*. Hillside, NJ: Enslow Publishers, 1991.

2. Bates, R. L., *Industrial Minerals: How They Are Found and Used*. Hillside, NJ: Enslow Publishers, 1987.

3. Bates, R. L., *Stone, Clay, Glass: How Building Materials are Found and Used*. Hillside, NJ: Enslow Publishers, 1987.

4. Bates, R. L., and J. A. Jackson, *Dictionary of Geological Terms*, Third Edition. New York: Anchor Press/Doubleday, 1984.

5. Bates, R. L., and J. A. Jackson, *Our Modern Stone Age*. Los Altos, CA: William Kaufman, Inc., 1982. Available from American Geological Institute, Alexandria, VA.

6. Bickel, Lennard, *The Deadly Element: The Story of Uranium*. Briarcliff Manor, NY: Stein & Day, 1980.

7. Blakey, A. F., *The Florida Phosphate Industry: A History of the Development and Use of a Vital Mineral*. Cambridge, MA: Harvard University Press, 1973.

8. Fodor, R. V., *Gold, Copper, Iron: How Metals Are Formed, Found, and Used*. Hillside, NJ: Enslow Publishers, 1988.

9. Green, Timothy, *The New World of Gold*. New York: Walker & Co., 1985.

10. Green, Timothy, *The World of Diamonds*. New York: William Morrow & Co., 1981.

11. Kesler, S. E., *Our Finite Mineral Resources.* New York: McGraw-Hill, 1976.

12. Multhauf, R. P., *Neptune's Gift: A History of Common Salt.* Baltimore: Johns Hopkins Press, 1978.

13. Pampe, W. R., *Petroleum: How It Is Found and Used.* Hillside, NJ: Enslow Publishers, 1984.

14. Weiss, S. A., *Manganese: The Other Uses.* London: Metal Bulletin Books, 1977.

BOOKLETS AND REPORTS

15. Dorr, Ann, *Minerals—Foundations of Society*, Second Edition. Alexandria, VA: American Geological Institute, 1987.

16. Ellison, S. P., Jr., *Sulfur in Texas.* Austin: Texas Bureau of Economic Geology, Handbook 2, 1971.

17. Fuzesy, A., *Potash in Saskatchewan,* Regina. Saskatchewan Geological Survey, Report 181, 1982.

18. *The Mineral Position of the United States—1987.* Washington, DC: U.S. Department of the Interior, 1988.

19. Taylor, G. C., *California's Diatomite Industry*, California Geology (Sacramento), vol. 34 (1981), pp. 183–192.

COMPUTER SOFTWARE

20. GlyDict, *Dictionary of Geology, Mining, and Related Terms.* Version 2.0, 1987, to be used as a supplemental dictionary with a word processor's spelling checker. Over 8,500 terms on a standard 5-1/4-inch IBM-PC–compatible disk. Available from Exploration Software, 150 Moss-Side Drive, Athens, GA 30607. Phone (404) 353-2492.

ABOUT THE AUTHOR

Robert L. Bates is Professor Emeritus of Geology at Ohio State University. He is a founder of the annual Forum on Geology of Industrial Minerals.

Dr. Bates has written a number of articles and books and was editor of the *Dictionary of Geological Terms*. His young adult titles for Enslow Publishers include *Stone, Clay, Glass: How Building Materials Are Found and Used* and *Industrial Minerals: How They Are Found and Used*. He is also the author of *The Challenge of Mineral Resources* in the Environmental Issues Series.